WHAT TO DO WHILE YOU'RE STILL YOUNG

THE DECISIONS YOU MAKE NOW WILL SHAPE THE REST OF YOUR LIFE

ALICE TRUMAN

TOP ARTISTS 4U LLC

First Printing, 2026

ISBN

Paperback - 13: 978-1-968871-89-5

Ebook - 13: 978-1-968871-90-1

Top Artists 4 U LLC

15021 Ventura Blvd. #783 Sherman Oaks, CA 91403

TopArtists4U@gmail.com

TA4UPublications.com

CONTENTS

Disclaimer 5
Author's Note 7
Introduction 11
A Note Before You Begin 15
Part I 19

1. Life Doesn't Ask If You're Ready 21
2. Youth Is Your Greatest Advantage 26
3. The Window Nobody Tells You About 31
4. The Illusion of "I'll Figure It Out Later" 38
Part II 43
5. If You Don't Understand Money, It Will Control You 44
6. Jobs, Hustles, and Business - What They Don't Tell You 49
7. Credit - The System You're Already In 54
8. How to Use Credit to Build - Not Survive 60
9. Saving, Investing, and Starting Small 66
10. If You Don't Have a 401(k), Then What? 73
11. Taxes - The Money You Earn But Don't Keep 80
Part III 87
12. Insurance - The Thing You Think You Don't Need 88
13. The Truth About Buying a Home 95
14. Relationships, Marriage, and the Real Cost of Commitment 103
Part IV 111
15. The People Around You Are Shaping Your Future 112
16. Lifestyle Creep - The Trap That Feels Like Progress 119
17. Emergency Funds - Your First Line of Defense 127
18. Debt - The Weight You Don't Feel Right Away 135
19. Student Loans - The Debt You Signed For Before You Understood It 144
Part V 153
20. The Power of Consistency Over Time 154
21. Delayed Gratification - Choosing Later Over Now 162
22. Discipline vs. Motivation 171
Part VI 181
23. The Cost of Waiting 182

24. Where Most People End Up - And Why 190
25. The Life You Can Build If You Start Now 199
26. The Checklist - What to Do While You're Still Young 209

Final Thoughts 223
Resources 231
Glossary of Key Financial Terms 239
Your Action Checklist 253
About the Author 259
Also by Alice Truman 261

DISCLAIMER

This book is designed to provide general financial education and information for readers who are navigating the early stages of their adult financial lives. It is intended to inform, to build awareness, and to encourage intentional financial decision-making - not to serve as personalized financial, legal, tax, or investment advice.

The information contained in these pages reflects the author's research, perspective, and understanding at the time of writing. Financial laws, tax regulations, contribution limits, interest rates, program requirements, and other details referenced throughout this book are subject to change. Readers are encouraged to verify current information through official sources - including the IRS, the Consumer Financial Protection Bureau, and the U.S. Department of Education - before making financial decisions based on the content of this book.

Every individual's financial situation is unique. The strategies, frameworks, and general guidance presented here may not be appropriate for every reader's specific circumstances. Before making significant financial decisions - including those related to investing, retirement planning, taxes, insurance, credit, debt management, homeownership, or legal agreements - readers are strongly encouraged to consult with a qualified financial advisor, tax professional, or attorney who can evaluate their individual situation and provide advice accordingly.

The author is not a licensed financial advisor, certified financial planner, tax professional, or attorney. Nothing in this book should be construed as the establishment of a professional advisory relationship between the author and the reader. The author and publisher accept no responsibility or liability for any financial decisions made by readers as a result of the information contained in this book.

The characters and scenarios presented throughout this book are illustrative in nature. Any resemblance to specific individuals, living or deceased, is coincidental.

Reference to specific financial institutions, websites, tools, books, or other third-party resources does not constitute an endorsement of those resources, nor does it imply that those resources endorse the content of this book. The author receives no compensation for the mention of any specific product, service, institution, or publication referenced herein.

Read this book as what it is - a practical guide to building financial awareness early in life. Use it as a foundation. Build on it with professional guidance where your situation warrants it. And apply what you learn with the understanding that your specific circumstances will always require your own informed judgment.

AUTHOR'S NOTE

This book didn't come from a place of having everything figured out. It came from the opposite - from watching people I cared about struggle with things that could have been avoided, from conversations that happened too late, from the quiet frustration of realizing that the most important financial lessons most people ever learn arrive after the damage has already been done.

It came from asking one question that I couldn't stop thinking about: what would change for someone if they understood all of this before life required them to?

That question is why this book exists.

I am not a financial advisor. I am not a certified planner or a licensed professional of any kind. What I am is someone who became deeply committed to understanding how money, credit, debt, and financial decision-making actually work — not in theory, but in the real lives of real people navigating real circumstances without a roadmap.

What I found, consistently, was that the people who struggled most were not the ones who lacked intelligence or capability or work ethic. They were the ones who lacked early, clear, practical information about how the systems around them operated. They made decisions without understanding the consequences. They built habits without realizing where those habits were leading. They assumed they would figure things out later - and later arrived more expensive than they expected.

I also found that the people who built genuinely stable, flexible financial lives were rarely the ones with the highest incomes or the most exceptional advantages. They were the ones who understood the basics early, applied them consistently, and made intentional decisions long before the stakes were high enough to force their attention.

That gap - between those who understood early and those who didn't - is one that education, for the most part, has failed to close. Schools teach many things. How to manage credit, how to build savings, how taxes work for someone who earns independently, how the decisions made at 22 quietly shape the options available at 35 - these are not among them.

This book is an attempt to close that gap. Not comprehensively - no single book could do that - but meaningfully. Practically. In a way that gives you enough understanding, early enough, to make decisions that serve your future rather than decisions that simply respond to your present.

Everything in these pages is written for someone who is still in the window where the right habits, built now, have the most time to compound. That window is open longer than most people realize - but it does close. And the earlier you begin, the more of it you have.

If even one chapter changes one habit that changes one trajectory, this book has done what it set out to do.

I hope it does more than that.

Now - read it. Apply it. And build something you're proud of.

INTRODUCTION

You've probably heard the saying - *youth is wasted on the young.* Most people nod at that and move on. But stop and think about what it's actually saying. It means that by the time most people understand how to use their time, energy, and opportunity wisely, those things are already gone. The knowledge arrives late. The awareness comes after the mistakes. And the lessons that could have changed everything show up only after the consequences already have.

This book exists to change that for you.

What you're holding is not a motivational pep talk. It's not a collection of vague advice about believing in yourself or chasing your dreams. Those things have their place, but this isn't that book. This is a practical guide to the real mechanics of life - how money works, how credit works, how the decisions you make in your twenties quietly shape the choices you'll have in your thirties, forties, and beyond. It's the kind of information most people wish someone had handed them before life handed them the bill.

Here's the truth that most people learn the hard way: life doesn't wait for you to feel ready. It doesn't pause while you figure things out. It just keeps moving — and the longer you wait to pay attention, the more ground you have to make up later.

But here's the other side of that truth, and this one works in your favor: **time is your greatest asset right now.** Not money. Not connections. Not luck. Time. And if you learn how to use it correctly - before the pressure builds, before the mistakes pile up, before the patterns become hard to break - you can build a life that most people spend decades trying to reach.

That's what this book is about.

You're going to learn how to understand and build credit before it becomes a problem. You'll learn the difference between earning money and actually keeping it. You'll understand what it really means to save and invest - not in a complicated, overwhelming way, but in a way that actually fits your life right now. You'll learn about taxes, insurance, debt, and the kinds of decisions — relationships, homeownership, your environment — that most people make without fully understanding what comes with them.

More than anything, you're going to see how small decisions, made consistently over time, either build a strong future or quietly work against one.

None of this is meant to scare you. It's meant to equip you.

Because the goal isn't perfection. The goal is awareness - and awareness, combined with action, is more powerful than anything else you have access to right now.

You don't need to have everything figured out before you start. You just need to start paying attention while you still have the advantage of time on your side.

Most people don't fall behind because they weren't capable. They fall behind because no one showed them what to expect. This book is here to change that.

So as you read, don't just absorb - apply. Think about where you are right now. Think about where your current habits are taking you. And ask yourself, honestly, whether the decisions you're making today are building the life you actually want.

Because you are at a point in your life where your future is still open, still shapeable, and still yours to define.

The only question is - what will you do with it while you're still young?

A NOTE BEFORE YOU BEGIN

There is a good chance that someone has already tried to tell you some of what is in this book.

Not in these exact words. Not organized into chapters. Not with this level of detail or structure. But the core of it - the warnings about money, the reminders about time, the quiet urgency behind the advice to get serious before life forces you to - that has probably come from someone who already loves you.

A parent. A grandparent. An aunt or uncle. An older friend. Someone who watched you moving through life and felt something they couldn't quite put into words - a familiar recognition, the echo of their own younger self - and tried, in whatever way they knew how, to hand something useful back across the distance between where they are and where you are.

And there is also a good chance that you didn't fully receive it.
Not because you're careless. Not because you don't respect the people who were trying to help. But because that's how this works. That's how it has almost always worked. The young can hear the words without

yet being able to feel the weight behind them - because the weight only becomes real after you've carried it. And by the time you've carried it long enough to understand what the warning was actually about, you're the one standing on the other side, trying to say the same thing to someone younger who isn't quite ready to hear it either.

This is the cycle that produces the phrase you've probably heard more than once.

Youth is wasted on the young.

It doesn't come from bitterness. It comes from a very specific kind of grief - the grief of understanding something too late to change the outcome, and watching the same thing happen again in someone you care about. The older people in your life who say it aren't trying to make you feel behind. They're trying to give you what time didn't give them - the understanding early enough to use it.

They already lived the cost of not knowing.

And they're watching, hoping you won't have to.

But maybe that's not your story.

Maybe you didn't have that person. Maybe there was no one in your life who tried to pass this forward - no parent who sat you down, no grandparent who pulled you aside, no mentor who saw something in you and cared enough to say something before the lessons got expensive. Maybe you grew up without that voice. Without that guidance. Without anyone reaching back to offer what they'd learned before life required you to learn it yourself.
If that's where you are - that's okay.

It's more common than most people admit. And it doesn't mean you missed something that was owed to you. It just means the information is arriving now, through these pages, instead of through a conversation that never happened.

Either way - whether you've heard pieces of this before or whether this is genuinely the first time any of it is being laid out clearly for you - consider this book that voice.

The mentor who tells you what's coming before it gets there. The older person who has seen enough to know what matters and cares enough to say it plainly. The conversation that maybe happened too late, or never happened at all, now happening on purpose - for you, while you still have time to use it.

Because that's what this book is trying to be.

Not a lecture. Not a list of rules. Not another thing telling you what you already know you should do.

A voice that actually gives you the information. That treats you like someone capable of handling the truth about how life works. That says the things most people only say after the fact — after the mistake, after the consequence, after the moment when it would have actually helped to know.

So before you move into the chapters that follow, there is one thing worth asking yourself honestly.

Has someone already tried to tell you something you didn't fully receive? Or have you been moving through life without anyone telling you these things at all?

Either answer leads you to the same place.

Here. Now. With enough time still ahead of you to do something with what you're about to read.

The people who tried to tell you before were right.

And if no one tried - consider this the moment someone finally did.

Pay attention.

Not because someone is telling you to.

But because you're old enough now to understand why it matters - and young enough that understanding it can still change everything.

This is your chance.

Don't let it pass the way chances do when we don't recognize them for what they are.

Because one day you'll be the older person looking back.

And when that day comes, the only question that will matter is whether you listened - when someone finally told you the truth.

PART I

THE TRUTH ABOUT LIFE

1

LIFE DOESN'T ASK IF YOU'RE READY

There is a version of life that most young people imagine — one where things unfold gradually, where you have time to prepare before anything serious lands on your doorstep, and where the big responsibilities wait patiently until you feel ready for them.
That version isn't real.

Life doesn't operate on your timeline. It doesn't slow down because you're still figuring things out, and it doesn't send a warning before it introduces you to pressure, consequence, or responsibility. It simply arrives. And when it does, the only thing that determines how well you handle it is whether or not you were paying attention before it got there.

Take Jason. At 23, he felt like he had things under control. He had a steady job, money coming in regularly, and nothing that felt urgent. Saving wasn't really on his radar. Credit was something he figured he'd deal with later. Planning for the future felt like a conversation for a different version of himself - an older one, with more to plan for.

Everything seemed fine.

Then, within the same month, his car needed an expensive repair, an unexpected bill he'd been putting off became impossible to ignore, and another expense appeared out of nowhere. None of these things were catastrophic on their own. But together, they created a pressure he wasn't prepared for - because he had no cushion, no backup plan, and no room to absorb any of it.

So he did what most people do in that situation. He reached for credit.

At first, it felt like a solution. The immediate problem was handled, the pressure eased, and life went back to feeling manageable. But then came the monthly payments. Then the interest. Then the slow realization that what felt like a quick fix had quietly become a long-term obligation following him every single month.

That's how it happens.

Not in one dramatic moment, but step by step. Small decisions that seem reasonable in the moment begin stacking on top of each other until they've built something you didn't intend to build. And by the time most people recognize the pattern, they've already shifted from preparing to reacting - and reacting is a much harder place to operate from.

The comfort of early adulthood is one of the most misleading feelings you'll ever experience. When nothing is going wrong, it's easy to assume nothing will. When your bills are manageable and your lifestyle feels stable, urgency disappears. There's no signal telling you to pay attention, no alarm that something needs to change.

But the absence of a problem is not the same as the presence of preparation.

Most people move through this stage of life assuming they have more time than they actually do. They push important decisions to the back

of the line. They react to situations instead of getting ahead of them. And while that may feel easier in the short term, it creates a compounding effect - the longer you wait, the more difficult it becomes to catch up, and the more of your energy gets spent managing consequences instead of building something.
There is another way.

Instead of waiting for something to go wrong, you begin paying attention before it does. Instead of reacting to situations, you prepare for the ones you can already see coming. Not because you have to have everything figured out right now, but because the earlier you build awareness, the less it costs you later.

Some things in life are not surprises - they are simply delayed certainties. You will have financial responsibilities. You will face unexpected expenses. You will make decisions that have longer consequences than they first appeared to have. These are not rare events. They are part of life for virtually everyone. The only real variable is whether you meet them prepared or caught off guard.

That difference changes everything.

Think honestly about where you are right now. Are there areas you've been putting off? Things you know you should understand better but haven't made the time to learn? Are you assuming you'll deal with certain responsibilities later, without having a clear idea of when later actually is?

These questions aren't meant to create anxiety. They're meant to create honesty. Because honest awareness is where change begins.
If you're between 18 and 22, you're in one of the most valuable windows of your life. You have time to build awareness without pressure — time to learn, to make small adjustments, and to build habits that will quietly work in your favor for years. What you do now, even

in small amounts, can put you ahead in ways you won't fully appreciate until later.

If you're between 23 and 30, the window is still open - but it calls for more intention. The things you've been putting off need attention sooner rather than later. Not because disaster is coming, but because the sooner you address them, the easier it becomes to move forward with control instead of constantly playing catch-up.
Wherever you are, the principle is the same: **start now.**

You don't need a perfect plan. You don't need to fix everything at once. But you do need to take a step - one step toward understanding something you've been avoiding, one step toward building a foundation instead of waiting for pressure to force your hand.

Pay closer attention to your money. Learn how credit actually works. Save something instead of spending everything. Decide that you're no longer going to ignore the things you already know matter.

Because life is already moving.

It was moving before you picked up this book, and it will keep moving after you put it down. The only question worth asking is whether you're moving with it - or waiting until it forces you to.

You don't need to know everything right now.

But you do need to start paying attention.

Because life doesn't ask if you're ready.

It just shows up.

And the only thing standing between you and being prepared for it - is the decision to start before it arrives.

What To Do This Week: Take fifteen minutes and write down three financial decisions or responsibilities you have been putting off. For each one, answer this question honestly: not what you plan to do about it - but why you haven't yet. Is it because you don't know how? Because nothing has forced you to? Because later has always felt available?

Whatever the honest answer is, write it down. You are not looking for solutions yet. You are building the awareness that makes solutions possible. That awareness starts with being honest about what you have been avoiding and why.

2

YOUTH IS YOUR GREATEST ADVANTAGE

If someone offered you an asset worth more than money, more than connections, more than any opportunity you could stumble into - and then told you that most people throw it away without realizing it - you'd probably want to know what it was.

It's time.

Specifically, it's the time you have right now, while you're young, before life gets heavier and the margin for error gets smaller. Time is the one resource that multiplies everything else. It multiplies your good decisions and your bad habits. It multiplies what you build and what you ignore. It works quietly in the background, and most people don't notice what it's doing until it's already done it.

The challenge is that time doesn't feel valuable when you have a lot of it. It feels endless. Like something you can spend freely, delay with, and always make up for later. That feeling is one of the most expensive illusions of youth - because later always has a cost, and that cost grows the longer you wait to pay attention.

Marcus was 21 when he landed his first real job. Consistent income, real independence, and for the first time in his life, money that was actually his to direct. It felt good. He spent the way most people his age do - eating out, buying things he wanted, enjoying the freedom that came with earning. There was nothing reckless about it. It just felt normal.

Saving didn't feel necessary yet. Investing wasn't even on his radar. Credit felt like something he'd figure out when it actually mattered. Everything could wait, because nothing felt urgent, and urgency is usually what gets people moving.

By 28, his income had increased - but so had everything else. His expenses were higher, his responsibilities were more real, and unexpected costs hit harder than they used to. And when he looked back at those early earning years, he saw them differently than he had at the time. Not as years where nothing important was happening, but as years where something important could have been quietly building - and wasn't.

That realization is one of the most common experiences people have in their late twenties. Not regret over one big mistake, but a quiet understanding that the advantage they had early on was spent instead of used.

Here's what most people misunderstand about time: they think of it as something they have, rather than something that's actively working either for them or against them.

When you start early, time works for you. Small amounts of money grow. Small habits compound into strong patterns. Small mistakes are easy to recover from because you have room to adjust. You're not racing against anything - you're building gradually, which is exactly how strong things get built.

When you start late, the dynamic flips. Time starts working against you. What could have grown gradually now needs to grow quickly. What could have been a small correction becomes a larger overhaul. What could have been built with ease now requires effort just to catch up. You're no longer building - you're compensating.

That shift happens not because of one big decision, but because of many small delays that each seemed harmless in the moment.

This is where most people get the idea of youth wrong.

They think of it as a time to enjoy before responsibility arrives - and there's nothing wrong with enjoying it. But youth is also a financial and strategic advantage that has a very real expiration date. The window where small actions create outsized results, where mistakes are cheap to recover from, where you can build a strong foundation without feeling the pressure of time running out - that window exists right now, and it closes gradually as life gets more complicated.

You can enjoy your life and still be intentional. You can spend and still be aware. You can live fully in the present while quietly building something for the future. It's not about restriction. It's about recognizing that the two things are not in conflict - and that a small amount of awareness now is worth far more than a large amount of effort later.

The shift in thinking is simple but powerful: instead of only asking what you can do right now, you also begin asking what you can do right now that will still make sense later. That question changes the way you see your decisions.

If you're between 18 and 22, this is where your advantage is at its strongest. You don't need large amounts of money to begin. You need consistency. Even small amounts, set aside and managed well, can grow into something meaningful simply because you gave them time to do so. What feels insignificant today can become significant later -

not because you did something extraordinary, but because you started early enough to let time do the heavy lifting.

If you're between 23 and 30, your advantage hasn't disappeared - but it requires more deliberate action. The window hasn't closed, but it is narrowing. This is the time to correct what you've been putting off, to build structure where there hasn't been any, and to stop treating important decisions as things you'll get to eventually. The sooner you move, the more of your advantage you reclaim.

Wherever you are, the principle is the same: start where you are, use what you have, and do something - because doing something consistently is always better than waiting to do something perfectly.

At some point, you will look back at this period of your life. That's not a prediction - it's a certainty. And when you do, you will see it for what it actually was: an opportunity. One of the clearest, most powerful opportunities you will ever have to shape the direction of your life without the weight of compounded mistakes, compounded debt, or compounded delay pressing down on you.

The question won't be whether you had the opportunity.

The question will be what you chose to do with it.

Youth isn't just a stage of life.

It's a window.

And what you build inside that window - or don't build - will echo long after it closes.

What To Do This Week: Identify one area of your financial life where you have been treating time as unlimited - saving, investing, building credit, addressing debt, or anything else you have been meaning to start. Then calculate, as specifically as you can, what the delay has already cost you. Not in vague terms - in real ones. If you had started saving $100 per month a year ago, what would that account hold today? If you had begun paying down a specific debt six months ago, how much lower would the balance be? Make the cost of waiting concrete. Once you can see it clearly, the case for starting now makes itself.

3

THE WINDOW NOBODY TELLS YOU ABOUT

There is something happening around you right now that almost nobody will say directly.

Not because it's a secret. Not because the people around you don't know it exists. But because it's so woven into the way the world operates that most people accept it without examining it - and by the time they examine it, the moment has already passed.

Here it is.

When you're young, the world extends grace to you that it quietly withdraws later.

Lenders are more patient with a 22-year-old who doesn't understand credit than a 35-year-old in the same situation. Employers mentor young people more readily than they mentor older ones. Family members step in to help in ways they won't later - because later, they assume you should have figured it out. Friends loan money to a 21-year-old who is struggling that they won't loan to a 38-year-old in the same position.

There is a social safety net woven specifically around youth that most young people don't even know exists.
And most of them find out it's gone only after they've already lost access to it.

This is not a small thing.

It means that the window you are in right now is not just financially valuable - it is socially valuable in a way that cannot be replicated later. The mistakes you make now are more forgivable. The help you need now is more available. The patience the world extends to you now is something you will not be offered again at the same level, in the same way, for the same reasons.

And the reason most people don't realize this is simple - nobody announces when the grace period ends.

There is no letter. No conversation. No moment where someone sits down with you and says: the world is about to start holding you to a different standard. From here forward, people will assume you know what you're doing. From here forward, the help you used to be able to count on will come less readily. From here forward, struggling with the same things you struggled with at 21 will be interpreted differently - not as someone still figuring things out, but as someone who should have figured it out already.

It just changes. Quietly. And you feel it before you understand it.

Think about the phrases you've heard - or will hear - as you move further into adulthood.

You're a grown man now.

You're a grown woman now.

On the surface those phrases sound like acknowledgment. Like respect. Like the world recognizing that you've arrived somewhere real. But underneath them is something else entirely. They are the world's way of saying: the window in which we were patient with your not knowing has closed. You are now expected to know.

And the painful truth is that most people hear those phrases before anyone actually gave them the knowledge those words assume they have.

Because here is what nobody says clearly enough:

Being an adult in age and knowing how to function as an adult are two completely different things.

One happens automatically. The other has to be learned. And the world confers the first on schedule - on a birthday, at graduation, the moment you sign a lease or open a bank account or take your first real job - without waiting for the second to arrive with it.

You can look exactly like an adult. You can hold a job, pay rent, manage a schedule, handle the surface requirements of independent life — and still be operating without the deeper understanding of how money works, how credit builds, how the decisions you're making right now are quietly compounding into a future you haven't seen yet.

The appearance of adulthood is automatic.

The knowledge that makes adulthood actually work has to be acquired. And the window in which the world is most willing to help you acquire it is shorter than most people realize.

The second thing worth saying plainly is this.

Once you pass through youth, you don't return to it.

Every other resource in life has some path to recovery. You can earn more money. You can rebuild relationships. You can change careers, move cities, start over in ways that are difficult but possible. Most things that get lost or damaged can be worked toward again.

But you cannot go back and be 22 again with everything you now know.

The decisions made in this window don't just affect this window. They echo forward into every decade that follows. An older person's life is, in many ways, a living consequence of what they did or didn't do when they were young. The financial position they're in. The habits they're running. The options available to them. The weight they're carrying or the stability they're standing on.

That's not cynical. It's just true.

And the people who understood it while they still had access to the window are the ones who used it differently than everyone else.
Not because they were more disciplined. Not because they had more resources or more information or a clearer picture of the future. But because someone - a parent, a mentor, a book, a conversation that landed at the right moment - told them early enough that the social conditions surrounding youth are themselves an unrepeatable advantage.

The grace extended to you.
The help available to you.
The forgiveness built into the system for you.
All of it has an expiration date that nobody announces.

This is worth sitting with honestly - not as a source of pressure, but as a source of clarity.
Because clarity is what makes action feel worth taking before something forces it.

Look at the people around you who are older - a decade, two decades ahead of you. The ones who seem to move through life with stability and control, who have options and can make choices from a position of strength rather than scrambling. And the ones who are working just as hard but always responding to something, always managing a consequence of something decided earlier.

The difference between those two groups is rarely intelligence. It is rarely a single dramatic choice or a lucky break that explains everything.

Most of the time it is something quieter.

It is whether they used the window when they had it.

Whether they took seriously the things that felt optional when nothing was urgent. Whether they built the foundation before the pressure arrived to force them to. Whether someone told them - or they figured out on their own - that the grace the world was extending to them was temporary. That the help available to them had an expiration date. That the system was more patient with them right now than it would ever be again.

The ones who knew that - and acted on it - built something.
The ones who didn't found out later. And later, as this book will say more than once, has a way of arriving more expensive than expected.

You are in the window right now.

The grace is still extended. The help is still available. The world still sees you as someone in the process of becoming rather than someone who should have already arrived. The social safety net that surrounds youth - the one most people don't even know exists until it's gone - is still there.

The question is not whether you have it.

The question is whether you know you have it.

Because knowing changes everything.

It means you stop treating the patience of the world around you as a permanent condition and start treating it as the temporary gift it actually is. It means you stop assuming that the help available to you now will be available in the same way later. It means you stop leaving things for a future version of yourself who will be held to a higher standard with fewer people willing to help them meet it.
It means you start now.

Not because you have to.

Because you understand - maybe for the first time, stated this clearly - that the window you're in is real, that it is valuable in ways that go far beyond money, and that it will close the same way it opened.

Quietly.

Without announcement.

And you'll know it's gone because the world will start using different words with you.

Words that assume you already know.
Words that expect you to already have it together.
Words that signal - clearly, if not kindly - that the grace period is over.

The goal of this chapter - and this book - is simple.
Make sure that when those words arrive, they're right.

What To Do This Week: Find one person in your life who is at least ten to fifteen years older than you - someone whose life reflects the kind of stability you want for yourself. Ask them one question: *What do you wish someone had told you or helped you understand when you were my age?* Then listen. What they tell you is a direct window into what the world stopped offering to help them with once youth passed. That conversation is worth more than any chapter in any book - including this one.

4

THE ILLUSION OF "I'LL FIGURE IT OUT LATER"

There are phrases that sound reasonable on the surface but quietly do a lot of damage underneath. Phrases that feel like decisions when they're actually just delays dressed up in confident language.
"I'll figure it out later" is one of the most common — and one of the most costly.

It sounds responsible, even. It implies awareness. It suggests that you know something needs attention, and that you're simply choosing a more convenient time to deal with it. In the moment, that feels perfectly logical. You're young, you're busy, nothing is on fire, and whatever needs handling can certainly wait until life slows down a little.

The problem is that life doesn't slow down. And "later" is not a time on the calendar - it's a habit of postponement that compounds quietly until it becomes something you can no longer postpone.

Danielle was 24 when she had what looked, from the outside, like a pretty solid life. Steady income, manageable bills, enough freedom to feel like things were under control. She had heard the advice about saving and building credit and managing money responsibly. She understood, in a general way, that these things mattered.

She just didn't feel the urgency yet.

So she kept moving. She used credit when she needed flexibility, telling herself she'd pay it down later. She spent without much structure, assuming she'd get more serious when her income increased. She pushed financial learning to the back of her list because nothing was forcing her to move it to the front.

Months turned into years. Small delays became entrenched habits. The balances she planned to handle later grew larger than she realized, because interest doesn't wait for you to be ready. The financial cushion she planned to build later never got started, because there was always something more immediate to spend on. And because nothing catastrophic happened to force a correction, the pattern continued - right up until the moment it couldn't.

Then life shifted.

An unexpected expense arrived, followed quickly by another. The balances she had been meaning to address suddenly demanded attention all at once. The cushion that wasn't there couldn't absorb any of it. And in that moment, she wasn't building anything. She was trying to recover from everything she hadn't built.

That's how "later" actually shows up.

Not as a calm, convenient pause where you finally have time to catch up. But as a moment where everything demands your attention simultaneously - and you're not in a position to give it.

Here's what makes this pattern so hard to break: the consequences of delay are invisible in the beginning. You make a decision to put something off, and nothing bad happens. You make the same decision again, and still nothing. That absence of immediate consequence is what tricks people into believing that later will always be available - that the grace period is unlimited.

It isn't.

What you delay doesn't disappear. It accumulates. Interest grows. Habits deepen. Time passes. And the gap between where you are and where you need to be gets wider quietly, without announcement, until the day it becomes impossible to ignore.

By that point, you're no longer in a position to prepare. You're in a position to repair. And repairing almost always costs more - more time, more money, more energy - than preparing would have.

Most people don't choose this path intentionally. Nobody sits down and decides to fall behind. What they do instead is make a series of individually logical decisions that, taken together, create a pattern they never consciously signed up for. They delay because nothing is urgent. They postpone because there's no immediate consequence. They assume the future will provide a better moment to start.

But the future is built entirely on what the present does.

There is a different way to approach this - and it doesn't require overhauling your entire life overnight.

It starts with honesty. Honest awareness about what you've been putting off, what you don't yet understand, and where your current habits are actually taking you. Not judgment - just clarity. Because clarity is where change begins.

From there, the move is simple: instead of waiting for urgency to force your hand, you begin before it arrives. You start learning before you're required to. You start building before the pressure shows up. You handle small things while they're still small, so they don't become large things you're forced to handle under stress.

You don't have to start with everything. Start with one thing. Pick one area - money, credit, saving, taxes - and take one step toward understanding it this week. Not a perfect step. Not a complete overhaul. Just one intentional move in the right direction.

If you're between 18 and 22, this is where your opportunity is clearest. You have time to build awareness without pressure. You can experiment, adjust, and develop habits before the stakes get high. Starting now doesn't feel dramatic because nothing feels urgent - and that's exactly the point. Building before the pressure arrives is always easier than building under it.

If you're between 23 and 30, the time to close the gap is now. Not next month. Not when things settle down. The things you've been putting off are not going to become easier to address the longer you wait — they're going to become more expensive, more complicated, and more disruptive. Starting now, even imperfectly, is always better than waiting for a perfect moment that isn't coming.

"Later" is not a plan.

It is a delay with consequences attached to it. Some of those consequences are minor. Others are the kind that take years to work through. The tricky part is that you usually can't tell which is which until you're already living with the outcome.

What you can control is when you decide to pay attention.
Because here's the thing about later - it always arrives. The question is just whether you show up to it prepared or scrambling. Whether your habits have been building something for you, or whether you're standing in the middle of what they built without you.

The advantage you have right now is rare and temporary. You can act on it before it costs you anything. You can build before you're forced to. You can make "now" your strategy instead of "later."

And once you do that - once you remove the illusion that later is always available - something becomes very clear.

Later isn't coming to save you.
You have to build it.
And the only time you can do that is now.

What To Do This Week: Identify the one financial area you have been putting off the longest. Not the most comfortable one to address - the one you have genuinely been avoiding. Write down how long you have been meaning to address it and what you have told yourself in the meantime about why later was acceptable.

Then write down one specific action - not a plan, not an intention, one action - that you could complete this week to move it from pending to in progress. It does not have to be large. It has to be real. Do that one thing before the week is over and let it be the moment that "later" stopped being your strategy.

PART II

MONEY

5

IF YOU DON'T UNDERSTAND MONEY, IT WILL CONTROL YOU

Money is going to be one of the most constant forces in your life - whether you pay close attention to it or not.

It will shape your choices, define your options, determine your level of freedom, and influence nearly every major decision you make. You will earn it, spend it, need it, worry about it, and make sacrifices because of it. And yet, for something so central to how life actually works, most people are never clearly taught how to handle it. Instead, they learn through experience - which usually means through mistakes, through stress, and through consequences that could have been avoided with a little understanding applied a little earlier.

The result is that most people don't manage money. Money manages them.

Andre was 25 when his income reached a level that felt genuinely comfortable for the first time. He had worked hard to get there, and he allowed his lifestyle to reflect it. Better apartment. Newer car. More freedom to spend without checking his balance first. From the outside - and from the inside - it looked like progress.

But something quietly wasn't adding up.

Despite earning more than he ever had, he never seemed to have anything left. His expenses had expanded to match his income so naturally, so gradually, that he hadn't noticed it happening. Every dollar coming in was already spoken for before it arrived. When something unexpected came up, there was no cushion - just pressure and a decision about which bill could wait another week.

What he thought was progress had actually become a trap. He wasn't building anything. He was maintaining a lifestyle that required every dollar he earned just to stay in place. And the moment his income changed - even slightly - the whole structure became fragile.

That's when he understood something that changed how he looked at money entirely: earning more does not automatically create financial stability. The problem was never his income. The problem was his understanding.

This is the core truth that most people miss, and it's worth saying plainly: **it's not how much you make that determines your financial health - it's what you do with what you make.**

High income with no structure creates the illusion of wealth while building nothing. Low income managed with intention can build a foundation that holds. The number matters, but the habits matter more. And habits are formed long before the numbers get large.

Most people fall into a pattern without realizing it. They earn, they spend, and they repeat. Their lifestyle expands whenever their income does. They focus on what they can afford right now instead of what they could build over time. And because nothing feels wrong in the moment, the pattern continues - until it's been running long enough to become the structure of their entire financial life.

Breaking that pattern later is possible. But it's harder, more disruptive, and more costly than simply not building it in the first place.

There is a different way to think about money - and it starts with one simple shift in the question you ask yourself.
Most people ask: *"How much can I spend?"*

The better question is: *"What is this money doing for me?"*
That shift moves you from consumption to intention. It changes how you see your income - not just as something to use up, but as something to direct. And when you start directing money instead of simply spending it, the entire experience of having it changes.

Every dollar you earn has the potential to do one of three things: it can be spent, it can be saved, or it can be used to build something.

Spending gives you immediate satisfaction. Saving gives you stability and breathing room. Building - through investing, through developing skills, through creating something - gives you growth. None of these is wrong on its own. The problem comes when one of them dominates at the expense of the others.

The goal is balance - knowing when to do each, and being deliberate about it instead of just letting money flow wherever it naturally goes.

Understanding money doesn't mean becoming obsessed with it or turning every decision into a financial calculation. It means developing enough awareness to see clearly what's happening with your money so you can make intentional choices instead of passive ones.

That awareness starts with a few simple questions:

Do you know where your money is actually going each month - not in general, but specifically? If your income increased today, would your savings grow, or would your spending simply expand to match it? Are your current financial habits building something, or are they just maintaining your present lifestyle?

These aren't trick questions. They're diagnostic ones. And the answers tell you more about your financial future than your income does.

If you're between 18 and 22, this is where your financial identity begins to form. You may not be earning large amounts yet - but that's not the point. The point is how you think about money right now, at this level, with these habits. If you learn to manage small amounts with intention, you will be prepared to manage larger amounts the same way when they arrive. If you ignore it now, the same patterns that feel manageable at low income become much more difficult to break when the numbers are larger and the stakes are higher.

If you're between 23 and 30, your income is likely growing and your decisions are beginning to carry real weight. This is the time to take deliberate control of how your money is being used — not just earning it and hoping it stretches, but actively directing it toward something. The structure you build now will either support everything that comes next, or make it harder than it needs to be.

A practical place to begin is this: before you spend anything in a given month, decide in advance where your money is going. Not after the fact, not as a reflection - before. Give every dollar a purpose. Set aside your savings first, before it becomes available to spend. Know what your necessary expenses are. And then make conscious choices with what remains.

That one habit - deciding before spending, instead of tracking after - changes the entire dynamic. It puts you in the driver's seat instead of the passenger seat of your own financial life.

Because money, when you understand it, becomes a tool.

A tool you use to create stability. To build options. To create the kind of freedom that isn't dependent on your next paycheck showing up exactly when it's supposed to.

But when money isn't understood, it becomes something else entirely.

It becomes the thing that controls your decisions, limits your choices, and quietly runs your life while you're busy trying to keep up with it.

The difference between those two outcomes isn't luck.
It isn't income.

It's understanding - applied early enough to matter.
So start paying attention now.

Not because everything has to be perfect.

But because the sooner you understand what your money is doing, the sooner you can make it start working for you - instead of the other way around.

What To Do This Week: Write down every expense from the past 30 days - every single one. Then put each one into one of three categories: necessary, optional, or unplanned. Don't judge what you find. Just look at it clearly. This single exercise will tell you more about your financial habits than any advice ever could - and it gives you an honest starting point to build from.

6

JOBS, HUSTLES, AND BUSINESS - WHAT THEY DON'T TELL YOU

At some point, you're going to earn money. You may already be doing it. And when that happens, the conversation almost always centers on one thing - how much you're making.

But how much you make is only part of the story.

How you earn your money affects far more than just the number on your paycheck. It affects your stability, your flexibility, your tax responsibilities, your level of control, and ultimately, how your entire financial life is structured. Not all income is created equal, and understanding the differences early can save you from a lot of confusion, stress, and financial surprises down the road.

There are three primary paths most people take when it comes to earning — a traditional job, independent work, or building a business. Each one has real advantages. Each one comes with real trade-offs. And most people don't find out what those trade-offs are until they're already living with them.

Kevin was 22 when he landed his first full-time job. The consistency felt like a relief. He knew when he'd get paid, how much he'd earn, and what was expected of him. For the first time, his financial life had a rhythm - and that rhythm felt like security.

For a while, it was.

But a few years in, changes at work began affecting his hours. His income shifted in ways he hadn't anticipated, and what once felt rock solid suddenly felt uncertain. In that moment, he realized something important: his financial security wasn't really his - it belonged to whoever controlled his schedule. He had stability, but not independence. And when the stability was touched, everything built on top of it became unstable too.

Around the same time, his friend Marcus was taking a different route. No traditional job — just freelance work, project by project, client by client. The flexibility felt like freedom. Some months were strong. Others were slower. What Marcus hadn't fully accounted for, though, was the weight that came with that freedom. No automatic tax withholding. No employer benefits. No structured system to protect him when work slowed down. When a dry stretch hit, the pressure arrived immediately - because there was nothing between him and the gap.

Then there was Alicia, who had decided early on that she wanted to build something of her own. She started a small business, driven by the vision of being in control and creating something that could grow beyond her own hours. The early days were exciting. She was making decisions, setting direction, and building with her own hands. But over time, the reality of what she had taken on became clear. Every decision carried consequence. Every slow month was her problem to solve. Every mistake cost her directly. The freedom she had imagined came packaged with a level of responsibility she hadn't fully anticipated.

Three different paths. Three very different experiences. And one truth that all three of them had to learn in their own way:

Earning money and being financially secure are not the same thing.

This is where most people get tripped up. They assume that once the income is flowing, the rest takes care of itself. But income is just the starting point. What you do with it - how you structure around it, how you protect it, how you prepare for when it changes - is what actually determines whether you're building something solid or just staying afloat.

A traditional job offers consistency and structure, but it also creates dependence. Your income is tied to decisions made by someone else. Your hours, your raises, your job security - none of that is fully in your control. That doesn't make employment a bad choice. It makes it a specific kind of choice, with specific limitations worth understanding.

Independent work offers flexibility and autonomy, but it also creates variability. Your income can change month to month based on demand, availability, and factors outside your control. You are also responsible for things an employer typically handles - taxes, health insurance, retirement contributions, and cash flow management during slow periods. The freedom is real, but so is the responsibility that funds it.

Building a business offers the highest potential ceiling - but also the highest floor of responsibility. You're not just earning; you're operating. Every piece of the system is yours to manage. The upside is that you're building something that can grow beyond your own direct effort. The downside is that in the early stages, the weight of that is entirely on you.

None of these paths is better than the others in an absolute sense. What matters is that you understand what comes with the one you're on - so you can prepare for it instead of being surprised by it.

No matter how you earn your money, there are questions that every income earner needs to be asking - questions that most people never think to ask until a problem forces them to.

How consistent is my income, and what happens if it changes? Who is responsible for managing the taxes on what I earn - me, or someone else? Do I have benefits like health insurance and retirement contributions being handled, or is that entirely on me? If my income stopped or dropped tomorrow, how long could I manage without it?

These questions aren't meant to create anxiety. They're meant to create a clear picture of where you actually stand - because you can't build on ground you haven't assessed.

There's also one more thing most people aren't told, regardless of which path they're on: **multiple income streams are not just for the wealthy.** They're a form of protection. When your income comes from more than one source, a disruption in one doesn't take everything down. That could mean a side project alongside a full-time job. A skill you monetize occasionally while building your main career. A small investment that generates passive returns over time. It doesn't have to be complicated - it just has to exist.

Dependence on a single income source, no matter how stable it feels, is a vulnerability. The sooner you begin thinking about how to diversify, the more resilient your financial life becomes.

If you're between 18 and 22, this is your time to explore without over-committing. You may try different ways of earning - jobs, side projects, small ventures - and that's valuable. But more important than what you choose is what you observe. Pay attention to how money comes in on each path, what responsibilities come with it, and what it feels like when something disrupts it. That awareness, developed early, gives you an advantage that most people don't gain until they've already made costly mistakes.

If you're between 23 and 30, this is where structure becomes essential. You may already be working, building something, or managing multiple streams. Now is the time to make sure your income isn't just arriving - it's being managed in a way that creates real stability. That means thinking beyond today, preparing for slower periods, and building systems that protect you when things don't go according to plan.

At the end of the day, the path you take to earn your money matters less than the awareness you bring to it.

Because the goal has never been to simply earn.

The goal is to build something that lasts - something that doesn't collapse the moment the income shifts, something that isn't held together entirely by the next paycheck showing up on time.
That kind of stability isn't built by earning more.

It's built by understanding what you have, protecting it intelligently, and making sure that no matter how your money comes in - it's working for you once it arrives.

What To Do This Week: Look honestly at your current income source and ask yourself two questions: What would happen if this income stopped or decreased by 30% tomorrow? And what is one skill, service, or asset you already have that could eventually become a second source of income - even a small one? You don't need to act on it immediately. You just need to start thinking about it now, before you need to.

7

CREDIT - THE SYSTEM YOU'RE ALREADY IN

Here's something most people aren't told when they're starting out: you don't have to apply for anything, sign anything, or make a single financial decision to already be affected by the credit system. The moment you begin interacting with money in certain ways - through a bank account, a bill in your name, a loan, or a credit card - you begin building a financial reputation. That reputation is tracked, measured, and used by lenders, landlords, employers, and institutions to decide how much trust to extend to you.

This system is called credit. And most people enter it without understanding how it works - which means most people spend years being shaped by it before they ever think to take control of it.

Brandon was 20 when he received his first credit card offer in the mail. It felt like a milestone - like the financial world was finally acknowledging that he existed. Approval meant access, and access felt like opportunity. He didn't think of the card as borrowed money. He thought of it as a tool that was now available to him.

In the beginning, his usage was small. A few purchases here and there. The minimum payment was low, the balance was manageable, and nothing about the situation felt like a concern. So the pattern continued - and gradually, expanded.

When money felt tight, the card filled the gap. When something came up that he hadn't planned for, the card made it possible. And because nothing negative happened immediately, the behavior kept reinforcing itself. Everything seemed fine.

Then the balance grew to a point where it stopped feeling manageable.

The minimum payments increased. Interest charges began appearing that he hadn't paid close attention to before. What once felt like flexibility began to feel like weight - something that followed him every month, required a portion of his income every month, and grew a little more expensive every month he didn't pay it down completely.

What he thought was helping him had been quietly working against him the entire time.

That's how most people first experience credit - not as a problem, but as a convenience. It feels accessible and easy to manage, right up until the long-term effects begin to surface. And by the time they do, the situation is no longer about learning how credit works. It's about dealing with what was already built without that understanding.

Let's be clear about what credit actually is, because the confusion around this single point causes more financial damage than almost anything else.

Credit is not free money. It is borrowed money - and everything you borrow is expected to be repaid, usually with additional cost attached.

That additional cost is interest. And interest is not a flat fee - it compounds over time, meaning it grows on top of itself the longer a balance remains unpaid. What looks like a manageable monthly payment on a high balance can end up costing significantly more than the original purchase by the time it's fully paid off. Most people don't do that math when they're swiping the card. They look at the monthly minimum and decide that's the cost. It isn't. The real cost is almost always higher - sometimes much higher.

Understanding this one fact changes how you look at every credit decision you make.

Beyond the mechanics of borrowing and repaying, there's a larger system at work - one that's tracking your behavior whether you're paying attention to it or not.

Every time you make a payment, miss a payment, open a new account, carry a high balance, or apply for new credit, that information is being recorded. Over time, those records form your credit history - a detailed picture of how you've managed financial obligations. That history gets distilled into a number, commonly known as a credit score, and that number follows you into some of the most important decisions of your adult life.

Want to rent an apartment? Your credit will likely be checked. Want to finance a car? Credit check. Apply for a mortgage, a business loan, certain jobs, or even some utility accounts? Credit check. The score itself isn't just a number - it's a signal that tells institutions how reliably you follow through on your commitments. A strong score opens doors. A weak one closes them, or makes the ones that stay open significantly more expensive.

And here's what makes this so important to understand early: **your credit history is being built right now, whether you're building it intentionally or not.** Every decision you make - or don't make - is contributing to that record. The only question is whether you're shaping it deliberately or leaving it to chance.

Most people approach credit the wrong way from the start. They think about access - if they're approved for a certain amount, they assume that amount is available to use. They spend based on what the limit allows rather than what their actual financial situation supports. And because the consequences aren't immediate, the pattern continues until it becomes a problem.

The shift that changes everything is moving from an access mindset to a responsibility mindset.

Access asks: *Can I use this?*

Responsibility asks: *Can I repay this without creating a problem for myself down the line?*

Those two questions lead to completely different decisions. And those decisions, made repeatedly over time, lead to completely different outcomes.

If you're between 18 and 22, this is where your credit foundation begins. You may be just entering the system, or you may already have an account or two. Either way, this is your opportunity to build correctly from the start - before habits form that are difficult to break. Starting small, keeping balances low, paying on time, and treating credit as a responsibility rather than a resource will put you in a position that most people spend years trying to reach.

If you're between 23 and 30, your focus should be on taking control of what's already been built. You may have accounts, balances, and a credit history that's been developing - for better or worse. This is the time to make sure your behavior is aligned with where you want your financial life to go. That means paying consistently, managing your balances carefully, and stopping the cycle of using credit to handle situations you weren't prepared for - because that cycle, if left unchecked, is one of the most effective ways to quietly limit your options for years.

Think honestly about how you currently view credit. Do you see it as something to use freely when it's convenient, or as something to manage carefully because it's always being measured? Are your decisions based on what you have access to, or on what you can realistically handle and repay?

Those aren't rhetorical questions. They're the questions that separate people who use credit as a tool from people who spend years being controlled by it.

Because when credit is understood and managed well, it genuinely opens doors. It supports your ability to make major moves - financing a home, building a business, handling genuine emergencies - without being shut out or charged a premium for your history.

But when it's used without understanding, it does the opposite.

It limits your options.

It creates monthly obligations that eat into your income for years.

It quietly closes the doors you were counting on being open.

And the difference between those two outcomes has nothing to do with how much money you make or how smart you are.

It has everything to do with how early you decided to pay attention.

So pay attention now.

Learn how the system works.

Use it carefully.

Build it intentionally.

Because once you understand credit - really understand it - you stop being someone the system happens to.

And you start being someone who uses it with purpose.

8

HOW TO USE CREDIT TO BUILD - NOT SURVIVE

There's a difference between knowing that credit matters and knowing how to use it in a way that actually works in your favor. Most people land somewhere in the middle - they're aware that credit exists, they understand in a general sense that it affects their financial life, and they try not to completely ignore it. But awareness without strategy is not enough. And for most people, the gap between what they know and what they actually do is exactly where the damage happens.

Using credit to survive means relying on it when things get tight, carrying balances because paying them off isn't realistic right now, and making minimum payments while the interest quietly grows in the background. It feels like managing. It isn't. It's maintaining - and maintaining a cycle that costs more the longer it runs.

Using credit to build is something entirely different. It means treating credit as a tool with a specific purpose, managing it with enough discipline that it works for you rather than against you, and understanding the mechanics well enough to make decisions that strengthen your financial profile over time.

The difference between those two approaches isn't income. It's understanding.

Jasmine was 22 when she got her first credit card shortly after starting her job. She had heard that paying on time was the most important thing, so she made sure she didn't miss payments. That part, she handled well. But beyond that, her understanding of how the system actually worked was limited - and that limitation quietly shaped every decision she made with the card.

She began to see her credit limit as something she could use freely, as long as she kept up with payments. When expenses came up, she used the card. When she wanted something and didn't have the cash available, she used the card. She was always paying - she just wasn't always paying enough to make meaningful progress.

The balance stayed high. Interest kept accumulating. And even though she was doing what she thought was the right thing, she wasn't actually getting ahead. She had moved, without realizing it, from using credit as a tool to depending on it as a crutch. And a crutch, by definition, is something that holds you up - not something that moves you forward.

To use credit to build, you need to understand what's actually being measured. Your credit profile isn't random, and it isn't based simply on whether you pay or don't pay. It's built on a specific set of factors, each carrying its own weight. Understanding those factors is what separates people who manage credit well from people who manage it just enough to avoid obvious disaster.

Payment history is the single most important factor in your credit profile. It's the record of whether you pay your obligations on time - every time. One missed payment can have a real and immediate negative impact. A long, consistent record of on-time payments, on the other hand, is the foundation of a strong credit profile. If you do nothing else correctly, this must be done correctly. Set up automatic payments if you need to. Put reminders in your phone. Do whatever it takes - because this one factor carries more weight than anything else in the system.

Credit utilization is the second major factor, and it's one of the most misunderstood. Utilization refers to how much of your available credit you're using at any given time. Most people assume that as long as they're within their limit, they're fine. That's not how the system sees it. Using a high percentage of your available credit - even if you pay it off every month - signals financial stress to lenders. The general guideline is to keep your utilization below 30% of your total available credit. So if your credit limit is $1,000, you want to carry no more than $300 on that card at any point. Lower is better. The less of your available credit you use, the more control you appear to have - and the more positively it reflects on your profile.

Length of credit history is a factor that most young people underestimate. The longer your accounts have been open and in good standing, the stronger your profile becomes over time. This is one of the reasons closing old accounts - even ones you're no longer actively using - can sometimes work against you. Time is a component of your credit strength, and removing older accounts shortens the average age of your credit history. When in doubt, keep accounts open and simply manage them with a small, occasional purchase that gets paid off immediately.

Credit mix refers to the variety of account types in your profile. A combination of revolving credit - like credit cards - and installment loans - like a car loan or student loan - generally reflects better than a single type of account. This doesn't mean you should take on debt just to diversify. It means that over time, as your financial life develops naturally, a healthy mix contributes positively to your overall profile.

New credit inquiries happen every time you apply for a new credit account. Each application triggers what's called a hard inquiry, which can temporarily lower your score. One or two inquiries over a period of time is normal and has minimal impact. But multiple applications in a short period - especially if you're being declined - signals risk and can compound the damage. Be intentional about when and why you apply for new credit. Don't apply because an offer arrived in the mail. Apply when it makes strategic sense for your financial situation.

Negative marks - missed payments, accounts sent to collections, bankruptcies, or other derogatory information - can stay on your credit report for years and have a significant impact on your score during that time. The most important thing to understand about negative marks is that prevention is exponentially easier than correction. It is far simpler to protect your credit history than to repair it after damage has been done. Once something negative is on your report, time and consistent positive behavior are the primary tools for recovery - and both of those take longer than most people expect.

All of these factors come together to produce what's commonly known as your credit score - most often calculated using the FICO scoring model, which ranges from 300 to 850. A score in the mid-600s is generally considered fair. The 700s are good. The 740s and above open up the best rates and terms on loans, mortgages, and financing. But here's what matters most: **your score is not something you chase - it's something that reflects your habits.** Focus on the behaviors, and the number follows naturally.

A practical framework for building credit correctly is this: start with one account, keep the balance well below the limit, pay it in full every month if possible - or at minimum, always pay on time. Let time work in your favor. Don't open multiple accounts quickly. Don't carry high balances because the limit allows it. And check your credit report regularly - at least once a year - to make sure everything being reported is accurate. Errors on credit reports are more common than most people realize, and an inaccurate negative mark can drag your score down through no fault of your own.

You're entitled to a free credit report from each of the three major bureaus - Equifax, Experian, and TransUnion — once per year through AnnualCreditReport.com. Use it. Know what's on your report. Don't let the system track your history without you tracking it too.

If you're between 18 and 22, this is your opportunity to build correctly from the very beginning. You don't need a perfect score overnight. You need to establish the right habits now so that time and consistency do the heavy lifting for you. One well-managed account, treated with intention, can lay a foundation that serves you for decades.

If you're between 23 and 30, your focus should be on strengthening and correcting what already exists. If there are high balances, begin reducing them. If there are habits that have been working against your profile, begin replacing them. If you've had missed payments or other negative marks, the path forward is consistent positive behavior over time - because that's the only thing that genuinely repairs a credit history. There are no shortcuts, but there is a clear path, and it starts with the next decision you make.

Credit is always moving in one of two directions.

It is either building something that will open doors for you later - or it is accumulating damage that will quietly close them.

There is no neutral position.

Every payment you make, every balance you carry, every account you open or ignore is contributing to one of those two outcomes. The goal is to make sure you know which one your current habits are building - and to make deliberate adjustments if the answer isn't what you want it to be.

Because credit, used correctly, is genuinely powerful.

It is not just a score on a report.

It is access. It is options. It is the ability to move when opportunity arrives - to finance a home, to weather an emergency, to take a calculated risk - without being penalized for a past you didn't manage well.

That access is built quietly, over time, through decisions that seem small in the moment.

So make them carefully.

Make them consistently.

And make them with the understanding that what you're building right now will either be working for you or against you - for years to come.

What To Do This Week: Pull your free credit report at AnnualCreditReport.com and review it carefully. Look for any accounts you don't recognize, any missed payments that are being reported, and anything that doesn't accurately reflect your history. If you don't yet have a credit account, research one beginner-friendly option - a secured credit card or a credit-builder loan - and understand what's required before applying. Knowledge before action, always.

9

SAVING, INVESTING, AND STARTING SMALL

Most people believe that building a strong financial future requires a significant amount of money to get started. They picture large investment accounts, high incomes, and some future moment where everything finally aligns and they're able to do things the right way. Because that moment hasn't arrived yet, they wait. They tell themselves they'll start saving when they have more. They'll begin investing when things feel more stable. They'll get serious when there's actually something meaningful to work with.

But that moment rarely comes - not because the money never arrives, but because the habit was never built. And without the habit, more money doesn't create more savings. It just creates more spending at a higher level.

The truth is uncomfortable but important: **the amount you start with matters far less than the decision to start at all.**

Luis was 21 with a simple approach to money. Whatever came in, went out. Not recklessly - just normally. He covered what he needed, enjoyed what he wanted, and didn't think much beyond the current month. Saving felt like something for a later version of himself - one who made more money and had fewer things pulling at it. Investing felt like something reserved for people who already had wealth to work with, not something you started from scratch with small amounts.

So he waited.

His income did increase over the years. But so did his lifestyle. What once felt like small indulgences became standard expenses. What once felt optional became expected. And even though he was earning more than he ever had, he still wasn't saving - not because he couldn't, but because he had never built the habit, and a habit that was never built doesn't appear automatically just because the income grows.

Later had arrived. But nothing had changed.

That realization - that starting later doesn't automatically make things easier - is one of the most important things you can internalize before it costs you. Because saving and investing are not about having enough money. They are about doing something consistently with whatever money you have.

Here's where most people misunderstand the process, and it's a misunderstanding that costs them years.

They treat saving as something that happens with what's left over. They pay their bills, cover their expenses, spend what feels reasonable, and then save whatever remains at the end of the month - if anything remains. The problem with that approach is that something almost always fills whatever space is left. Life is very good at expanding to consume available resources. If saving is last in line, it rarely makes it to the front.

The correction is simple, but it requires a shift in how you think about your money the moment it arrives.

Save first. Spend what remains.

That single reversal changes everything. When saving comes out before you have access to the rest, it stops feeling like a sacrifice and starts feeling like a fixed cost - like rent or a utility bill, something that just happens as part of the normal flow. Over time, you stop noticing it's gone, and you start noticing what it's becoming.

Once the habit of saving is established, the next step is understanding how to make your money work beyond just sitting in an account.

That's where investing comes in - and this is the word that causes more unnecessary hesitation than almost any other in personal finance. Investing sounds complicated. It sounds risky. It sounds like something that requires expertise, large sums, and a level of financial sophistication that most people don't feel they have.

It doesn't.

At its core, investing is simply placing your money somewhere it has the potential to grow over time. That's it. The mechanics can become complex if you want them to, but the fundamental concept is straightforward - and the most important factor involved isn't how much you invest. It's how long you give it to grow.

This is where starting small becomes genuinely powerful.

When you invest early - even modest amounts - time does something remarkable. It allows growth to compound. Compounding means that the returns your money generates begin generating their own returns. It's growth building on growth, quietly and consistently, in a way that becomes increasingly significant the longer it runs. The difference between starting at 22 and starting at 32 isn't just ten years of contributions - it's ten years of compounding, which can represent a difference of tens of thousands of dollars by the time retirement approaches, even if the monthly contributions are identical.

This is not a technicality. It is the single most powerful argument for starting now, with whatever you have, rather than waiting for the right moment that may never feel quite right enough.

A practical framework for structuring your money is to think of every dollar you earn as having one of three destinations: living, saving, and building.

Living covers your actual life - your rent, your food, your transportation, your responsibilities, and yes, the things you enjoy. This is not the enemy. It is the point. You work so you can live.

Saving creates your cushion - money set aside for stability, for unexpected situations, for breathing room. This is what protects you when life doesn't go according to plan, which it regularly won't.

Building is where your money goes to grow - contributions to an investment account, a retirement fund, or any vehicle designed to increase your wealth over time rather than simply preserve it.

A simple starting split might look like this: 70% toward living expenses, 20% toward saving, and 10% toward building. If that feels like too much too soon, adjust it. Even an 80/10/10 split - 80% living, 10% saving, 10% building - creates meaningful momentum over time. The exact percentages are less important than the principle behind them: every dollar has a direction, and that direction is decided in advance.

The next step is to make the process automatic.

Don't rely on motivation or discipline to move money into savings and investments each month. Motivation is inconsistent and discipline is exhaustible. Systems are neither. Set up automatic transfers so that a portion of every paycheck moves into savings before you have the opportunity to spend it. Set up recurring contributions to an investment account so that building happens in the background without requiring a decision every single month. When the right behavior is automated, you stop having to choose it - it simply happens.

When it comes to investing, the goal at this stage is not to find the fastest-growing option or to time the market or to chase returns. The goal is to participate consistently in something that grows steadily over time. For most people starting out, this means low-cost index funds - investment vehicles that track the overall performance of the market rather than trying to beat it. They are simple, widely available through most brokerage accounts and retirement plans, and have historically provided strong long-term returns without requiring active management or expert knowledge.

You don't need to master the intricacies of the stock market to begin investing effectively. You need to open an account, contribute consistently, choose broadly diversified options, and leave it alone. Time and consistency do the rest.

If you're between 18 and 22, your advantage here is the strongest it will ever be. The amounts don't need to be large. They need to be consistent. Even $25 or $50 a month invested early has the potential to grow into something significant by the time you reach your forties and fifties - not because the amount is impressive, but because the time is. What feels like a small decision right now can become one of the most financially significant decisions of your life simply because you made it early enough.

If you're between 23 and 30, the window is still wide open - but it calls for more intentional action. If you haven't started yet, start now. Not with pressure, and not with the need to catch up all at once, but with consistency. Set aside something this month. Open an account this week. Make one move in the right direction and then build from there. The sooner you begin, the more of the compounding benefit you capture.

Take an honest look at your current habits. Are you saving consistently, or only when something happens to be left over? If your income increased tomorrow, would your savings grow - or would your lifestyle simply expand to match it? If nothing changed about the way you currently manage your money, what would your financial position look like in five years?

These questions are not meant to make you feel behind.

They're meant to help you see clearly - because clarity is the only starting point that actually leads somewhere.

You don't need to do everything at once. You don't need a perfect system on day one. You need to start somewhere, stay consistent, and trust that small actions done regularly are never as small as they feel in the moment.

Because the most powerful financial tool available to you right now isn't a specific investment or a high income or a lucky opportunity.

It's time.

And the only way to use it is to start before you feel ready.

Start small.

Save first.

Build consistently.

And let time do what it does better than anything else -

turn small, intentional decisions into something that changes your life.

What To Do This Week: Open a dedicated savings account if you don't already have one - separate from your everyday checking account. Decide on a fixed amount, however small, to transfer into it on the same day every week or every payday. Then research one beginner-friendly investment account - a Roth IRA through Fidelity, Vanguard, or Schwab is a strong starting point for most people - and understand what's required to open one. You don't have to fund it this week. You just have to know what the next step looks like.

10

IF YOU DON'T HAVE A 401(K), THEN WHAT?

For a long time, the standard picture of retirement planning looked like this: you get a job, your employer offers a 401(k), you contribute a portion of each paycheck, your employer may match some of it, and over decades that account grows into a meaningful piece of your financial future. It was a system built around a particular kind of employment - stable, long-term, with benefits - and for people who fit that mold, it worked reasonably well.

But the workforce has changed significantly. More people are freelancing, contracting, building their own businesses, or working for smaller employers who don't offer retirement benefits. Others are working multiple part-time jobs, none of which come with structured plans. And many young people are simply in the early stages of careers where retirement planning feels distant and abstract - something to figure out later, when life is more settled.

The problem with that thinking is the same problem that runs through every chapter of this book.

Later is expensive.

And when it comes to retirement specifically, the cost of waiting isn't just financial - it's mathematical. Every year you delay is a year of compounding growth that you cannot recover. Not through larger contributions, not through better investments, not through any strategy available to you. The time simply doesn't come back.

So the question isn't whether you have a 401(k).

The question is whether you are doing anything at all to prepare for a future where your body may not be able to work, where you may not want to work, or where the work simply may not be available.

Darren was 26 and doing well on his own terms. He had built a steady freelance income, worked independently, and valued the flexibility that came with not being tied to a traditional employer. What he didn't have - and hadn't thought much about - was any kind of structure for his future. No retirement account. No automatic contributions. No plan beyond earning what he needed now and figuring the rest out later.

For a while, that felt fine.

He was young. His income was growing. Retirement felt like a problem for a much older version of himself — one who would presumably have more resources and more clarity about how to handle it.

But as time passed, something began to feel off.

He was working consistently, earning steadily, and building a comfortable present - but nothing was accumulating for his future. If he stopped working, the income stopped with it. Entirely. There was no account quietly growing in the background. No safety net building itself while he focused on the present. Just income that arrived, got used, and reset to zero at the beginning of every new month.

That realization - that earning money and preparing for the future are not the same activity - is where this chapter begins.

A 401(k) is not magic. It is a structure - a system designed to make retirement saving automatic, tax-advantaged, and consistent. What makes it powerful is not the account itself, but the behavior it produces: regular contributions, long time horizons, and the discipline of treating retirement savings as non-negotiable.

If you don't have access to a 401(k), you don't have the automatic structure. But you can build your own. And in some ways, building your own gives you more flexibility and more control than an employer-sponsored plan would.

The most accessible and powerful option for most people without a 401(k) is an **Individual Retirement Account - commonly known as an IRA.** There are two primary types, and understanding the difference between them is important.

A **Traditional IRA** allows you to contribute money before it's taxed, which reduces your taxable income now. You pay taxes on the money when you withdraw it in retirement. This can be advantageous if you expect to be in a lower tax bracket in retirement than you are today.

A **Roth IRA** works in the opposite direction. You contribute money that has already been taxed, and in return, your money grows completely tax-free. When you withdraw it in retirement, you owe nothing in taxes - not on the contributions, and not on decades of growth. For most young people who are currently in a lower income bracket and expect their earnings to increase over time, the Roth IRA is generally the stronger choice. You pay taxes now, at your current lower rate, and let everything that grows from that point forward remain yours entirely.

For 2024, the contribution limit for both Traditional and Roth IRAs is $7,000 per year if you're under 50. That breaks down to $583 per month - but you don't need to hit that number to start. You can open a Roth IRA with as little as $1 at some brokerages, and contribute whatever amount fits your current situation. The habit matters more than the amount, especially in the beginning.

If you are self-employed or running your own business, there are additional options beyond the standard IRA that allow for significantly higher contribution limits.

A **SEP-IRA** - Simplified Employee Pension - allows self-employed individuals to contribute up to 25% of their net self-employment income, up to a much higher ceiling than a standard IRA. It's straightforward to set up, has no complex administrative requirements, and can be a powerful vehicle for someone with variable income who wants to contribute more in strong earning years and less during slower ones.

A **Solo 401(k)** - sometimes called an Individual 401(k) - is designed for self-employed individuals with no employees other than a spouse. It allows you to contribute both as an employee and as an employer, which means the contribution limits are significantly higher than a standard IRA. For someone with a growing self-employment income who wants to maximize their retirement savings, the Solo 401(k) is worth serious consideration.

You don't need to understand every detail of these options to take action. What you need to understand is that options exist - and that the absence of an employer-sponsored plan is not an excuse to do nothing. It is simply a reason to take personal responsibility for building the structure yourself.

Regardless of which account type fits your situation, the approach to building it effectively follows the same principles.

Create separation. Open a dedicated retirement account and treat it as entirely separate from your everyday finances. The money that goes into this account is not available to spend. It is not an emergency fund. It is not a backup for when things get tight. It exists for one purpose - your future. Without that separation, it becomes too easy to rationalize using it for present needs.

Commit to consistency. Decide on a percentage of your income - not a fixed dollar amount, but a percentage - that will go into your retirement account regularly. A percentage adjusts automatically as your income changes. Ten percent is a strong starting target. If that's not immediately possible, start with five and build from there. The habit of consistent contribution is more valuable than the amount, especially early on.

Automate the process. Most brokerages allow you to set up recurring contributions that move money automatically on a schedule you choose. Use this feature. Remove the monthly decision from your plate entirely. When retirement saving happens automatically, it becomes part of your financial infrastructure rather than something you have to choose to do over and over again.

Leave it alone. This is harder than it sounds. Markets go up and markets go down, and when they go down - sometimes sharply - the instinct is to panic and pull money out. Don't. Retirement accounts are long-term instruments. Short-term volatility is normal, expected, and largely irrelevant if you have decades before you need the money. The accounts that grow into something meaningful are the ones that were left alone long enough for time and compounding to do their work.

If you're between 18 and 22, starting a retirement account right now - even with a very small amount - is one of the highest-return decisions available to you. Not because the amount will be large, but because the time you're giving it is extraordinary. Money invested at 21 has potentially four decades to compound before it's needed. That kind of time horizon is something you can never buy back, no matter how much you earn later.

If you're between 23 and 30, the urgency becomes more real with every passing year. Not in a way that should create panic - but in a way that should create action. Every year you delay is a year of compounding that belongs to someone else's financial future, not yours. Opening an account this month and contributing something - anything - is categorically better than waiting for a more convenient moment that may never arrive.

Think honestly about your current situation. If your income stopped completely tomorrow, how long could you sustain your life without it? Are you building anything that will support you when you're no longer able or willing to trade your time for money? If you worked at your current pace for the next thirty years and saved nothing along the way, what would the end of that road look like?

These questions aren't meant to be frightening.

They're meant to be clarifying.

Because the goal of retirement planning isn't to think about being old. It's to think about being free - free from the requirement to work because you need to, free to make choices based on what you want rather than what you can afford, free to have options when life changes in ways you didn't plan for.

That freedom is built quietly, over time, through consistent contributions to accounts that most people don't pay close enough attention to until they wish they had started sooner.

You don't need an employer to do this for you.

You need a decision, an account, and the discipline to contribute consistently.

That's it.

The rest is time.

And right now, time is still on your side.

What To Do This Week: Research opening a Roth IRA through one of the major low-cost brokerages - Fidelity, Vanguard, or Schwab are all strong options with no account minimums and no annual fees. Understand the contribution limits, the income eligibility requirements, and what the process looks like to open one. If you're self-employed, spend fifteen minutes reading about the SEP-IRA or Solo 401(k) to understand which fits your situation better. You don't have to open the account this week - but you should know exactly what it takes so that when you're ready to move, there's nothing standing in your way.

11

TAXES - THE MONEY YOU EARN BUT DON'T KEEP

There is a moment that catches almost everyone off guard at least once - usually early in their working life, and almost always at the worst possible time. It's the moment you realize that the money you earned is not entirely yours to keep.

For some people, it shows up the first time they look closely at a pay stub and notice how much has been deducted before the check ever reaches them. For others, it arrives as a bill from the IRS at tax time — a number they weren't expecting, representing money they had already spent. Either way, the realization lands the same way: somewhere between confusion and frustration, with a strong undercurrent of wishing someone had explained this earlier.

Taxes are not a surprise that appears out of nowhere. They are a permanent, predictable part of your financial life - one that begins the moment you start earning money and follows you in one form or another for the rest of your working years. The people who experience them as a disruption are the ones who never built them into their plan. The people who experience them as manageable are the ones who understood how they worked before they were forced to.

The goal of this chapter is to make sure you're in the second group.

Malik was 24 when he started picking up freelance work alongside his part-time job. The additional income felt like real progress - more money coming in, more flexibility, more options. And because freelance payments came directly to him with nothing taken out, it felt like he was earning more than ever before. Every payment arrived in full. Every dollar felt available.

So he used it.

He covered expenses, enjoyed his life, and treated the extra income the way most people treat unexpected money - as a bonus with no strings attached.

Then tax season arrived.

For the first time, he sat down with his income numbers and realized that a significant portion of what he had earned throughout the year was not actually his to keep. The taxes on his freelance income - income that had arrived in full, with nothing withheld - were now due all at once. And because he hadn't set anything aside, he didn't have it. What had felt like extra money all year had actually been borrowed time. The bill had simply been deferred until April.

That experience - common, avoidable, and expensive - is the direct result of not understanding how taxes work before they work against you.

To understand taxes, it helps to first understand why some people are caught off guard by them and others aren't.

When you work a traditional job as an employee, your employer withholds taxes from each paycheck before you ever see the money. Federal income tax, state income tax where applicable, Social Security, and Medicare - all of it gets pulled out in advance and sent directly to the government on your behalf. By the time your paycheck arrives, the tax obligation has already been partially or fully handled. This is why most traditional employees either owe a small amount or receive a refund at tax time - the withholding throughout the year was close to what they actually owed.

When you earn money independently - through freelance work, self-employment, a side business, or contract work - none of that automatic withholding happens. The payment arrives in full, and the tax responsibility is entirely yours to manage. This is where most people make the mistake Malik made: they treat the full amount as income available to spend, without accounting for the portion that was never really theirs.

The government still expects its share. The only difference is the timing - and if you haven't set anything aside, that timing creates a crisis.

There is one additional layer that catches self-employed people off guard, and it's important to understand it clearly.

When you work for an employer, your Social Security and Medicare taxes - collectively known as FICA taxes - are split between you and your employer. You pay half, they pay the other half. When you are self-employed, there is no employer to split the cost. You pay both halves yourself. This is called the **self-employment tax**, and it currently amounts to 15.3% of your net self-employment income, on top of your regular income tax obligations.

This is not a penalty for working independently. It is simply the full cost of a contribution that gets divided when an employer is involved. But it means that self-employed individuals need to set aside a higher percentage of their income than many people initially expect - because the total tax burden is larger than what most employees experience.

A practical rule of thumb for anyone earning independent income: **set aside between 25% and 30% of every payment you receive for taxes.** The exact amount will vary depending on your total income, your deductions, and your state's tax requirements - but setting aside that range consistently will protect you from owing more than you have at tax time. If you end up owing less, the difference stays in your pocket. If you set aside nothing and owe more than expected, you're facing a bill you can't pay - which carries penalties and interest on top of the original amount.

There is also the matter of **estimated quarterly taxes** - something that surprises nearly every first-time self-employed person.

When you earn independent income, the IRS expects you to pay taxes on that income throughout the year, not just at the end of it. This is done through quarterly estimated tax payments, due four times per year - typically in April, June, September, and January. If you earn significant self-employment income and don't make these payments, you may face an underpayment penalty on top of whatever you owe at tax filing time.

This doesn't have to be complicated. The simplest approach is to set aside your tax percentage with every payment you receive, keep it in a separate account that you don't touch for everyday expenses, and make the quarterly payments on schedule. The IRS website provides clear guidance and payment options, and most tax software walks you through the calculation process. The point is to be aware that this obligation exists - because most people aren't, until they're already behind on it.

Beyond the basics of withholding and quarterly payments, there are aspects of the tax system that actually work in your favor - if you know about them.

Deductions reduce the amount of your income that gets taxed. For self-employed individuals, many legitimate business expenses are deductible - things like a portion of your home if you work from it, equipment you use for work, software subscriptions, professional development, and more. Keeping organized records of these expenses throughout the year means you're not leaving money on the table when tax time arrives.

Retirement account contributions are another powerful tax tool. Contributions to a Traditional IRA or SEP-IRA reduce your taxable income for the year in which you make them. Contributing to retirement not only builds your future - it lowers your tax bill today. This is one of the clearest examples of how understanding the system can work in your favor rather than against you.

The standard deduction is available to everyone and automatically reduces the amount of your income subject to tax. For 2024, it stands at $14,600 for single filers. If your deductible expenses don't exceed that amount, you take the standard deduction automatically - no itemization required.

You don't need to become a tax expert to benefit from these provisions. You need enough awareness to keep organized records, ask the right questions, and work with a qualified tax professional when your situation warrants it. A good accountant or tax preparer doesn't just file your return - they help you understand what you owe, what you can reduce, and how to position yourself better for the year ahead.

Organization is the foundation of manageable taxes, and it costs nothing to build.

Keep records of your income as it arrives. If you're self-employed, track every payment - who paid you, how much, and when. Keep records of your business expenses, with receipts or documentation to support them. Use a simple spreadsheet, a dedicated folder, or one of many available apps designed for exactly this purpose. The goal is to never arrive at tax season scrambling to reconstruct a year's worth of financial activity from memory. That scramble is stressful, expensive, and entirely avoidable.

If you work a traditional job and receive a W-2, your tax situation is simpler - but it still benefits from attention. Review your withholding periodically to make sure the right amount is being taken out. A significant life change - a raise, a second job, a major deduction - can affect how much you should be withholding, and adjusting it proactively prevents surprises in either direction.

If you're between 18 and 22, this is your opportunity to build the right habits from the beginning. You may be earning relatively small amounts right now, but the understanding you develop at this stage will serve you for the rest of your working life. Learn how taxes work before they become complicated. Set aside a portion of any independent income automatically. Don't spend money that isn't fully yours to spend.

If you're between 23 and 30, your income is likely growing and your tax situation is becoming more complex. This is the time to move beyond guesswork and build real structure around your tax obligations. If you've been earning independently without making quarterly payments or setting money aside, address that now — before the gap between what you owe and what you have grows any larger. And if you haven't worked with a tax professional, this may be the year to start. The cost of that guidance is almost always worth it.

Taxes are not going away. They are not optional, and they are not something you can outrun by simply not thinking about them. But they are also not the threat that most people treat them as - not when you understand how they work and build them into your plan from the beginning.

The people who experience taxes as a crisis are almost always the people who encountered them without preparation. The people who experience them as manageable are the people who understood what was coming and set themselves up accordingly.
That preparation doesn't require advanced knowledge or a financial background.

It requires awareness.

It requires the discipline to set aside what isn't fully yours.
And it requires the honesty to stop treating tax obligations as someone else's problem until they become impossible to ignore.
Because they will not ignore you.

They will arrive on schedule, every year, whether you are ready or not.

The only variable is whether you are.

What To Do This Week: If you earn any independent or freelance income, open a separate savings account specifically for taxes and transfer 25–30% of your most recent payment into it today. If you work a traditional job, pull up your most recent pay stub and identify exactly how much is being withheld for federal and state taxes. Then visit IRS.gov and spend fifteen minutes reading about estimated quarterly taxes so you understand whether that obligation applies to your current situation. Awareness before obligation - always.

PART III

YOUR LEGACY BEYOND PAPERWORK

12

INSURANCE - THE THING YOU THINK YOU DON'T NEED

There is a particular kind of financial vulnerability that feels invisible right up until the moment it isn't. It doesn't announce itself in advance. It doesn't give you time to prepare once it arrives. It simply appears - in the form of a medical bill, a car accident, a sudden inability to work, or any number of situations that nobody plans for precisely because they feel unlikely until they happen.

This is the vulnerability that insurance exists to address.
And yet, for most young people, insurance sits at the bottom of the financial priority list - below saving, below investing, below almost everything else that feels more immediate and more tangible. The logic is understandable: why pay for protection against something that probably won't happen? Why add another expense to a budget that's already stretched? Why deal with something that feels, at this stage of life, like a problem for older people with more to lose?

The answer is the same answer that runs through every chapter of this book.

Because by the time it feels necessary, it's already too late to prepare for it.

Nicole was 27 and finally hitting a stride she had worked hard to reach. Steady income, manageable bills, a routine that felt sustainable. She was aware that insurance existed - health coverage, life insurance, disability protection - but none of it felt urgent. She was young, healthy, careful, and not in a financial position where adding more monthly expenses felt justified. She would deal with it later, when she had more to protect and more resources to protect it with.

Then something unexpected happened.

A medical issue arose that required immediate attention - the kind that couldn't be managed with a doctor's visit and a prescription. Treatment took time. Recovery took longer. And the financial impact extended far beyond the medical bills themselves. Time away from work meant lost income. Additional expenses appeared that she hadn't anticipated. And because she had no coverage in place, every piece of it landed directly on her — on savings that weren't large enough to absorb it, on credit that shouldn't have been used for it, and on a recovery process that was made significantly harder by financial stress running alongside the physical one.

The medical situation was difficult enough on its own.

The financial situation made it worse than it ever needed to be.

That's what unprotected vulnerability looks like in practice. Not a theoretical worst-case scenario - a real one, experienced by real people with real consequences that last long after the original incident is resolved.

Insurance is one of those concepts that's easy to understand in principle but easy to dismiss in practice. So let's be clear about what it actually is and why it matters.

At its core, insurance is a financial tool that transfers risk. Instead of carrying the full weight of a potential catastrophic expense by yourself, you pay a regular, predictable amount - a premium - and in exchange, the insurance company absorbs the large, unpredictable cost if and when it occurs. You are trading certainty for protection. A known monthly expense in exchange for coverage against an unknown but potentially devastating one.

The reason this matters so much when you're young is the same reason most young people dismiss it: nothing has gone wrong yet. And nothing going wrong feels like proof that nothing will. But that logic doesn't hold up under scrutiny. The absence of a crisis is not evidence that a crisis isn't possible. It's simply evidence that one hasn't happened yet.

What insurance does is ensure that when something does happen - and statistically, something will at some point - it doesn't have the power to dismantle everything you've been working to build.

There are several types of insurance worth understanding, each covering a different category of risk.

Health insurance is the most critical for most people and the most urgent to address. Medical costs in the United States are among the highest in the world, and even a single hospitalization, emergency room visit, or serious diagnosis can generate bills that run into tens of thousands of dollars. Without coverage, those costs fall entirely on you. With coverage, they are shared - often dramatically reduced - through a combination of premiums, deductibles, and out-of-pocket maximums that cap how much you can be required to pay in a given year.

If you are under 26, you may still be eligible to remain on a parent's health insurance plan - check whether that option is available to you. If you are employed, your employer may offer a group health plan, often at a subsidized cost that makes it significantly more affordable than purchasing coverage independently. If neither of those options applies, health insurance is available through the federal marketplace at HealthCare.gov, where plans are offered at various coverage levels and income-based subsidies may reduce your premium substantially. The key is to have something in place - not the most comprehensive plan available, but a baseline of protection that prevents a medical situation from becoming a financial catastrophe.

Disability insurance is the most overlooked form of coverage among young people, which is particularly ironic because young people are exactly who it's designed to protect. Disability insurance replaces a portion of your income - typically between 60% and 70% - if you become unable to work due to illness or injury. Your ability to earn an income is your most valuable financial asset at this stage of your life. Everything you're building depends on it. Disability insurance protects the asset that funds everything else.

Short-term disability coverage typically kicks in after a brief waiting period and covers you for weeks to months. Long-term disability coverage addresses extended periods of inability to work - months to years, or in some cases permanently. If your employer offers disability coverage, understand what it provides and whether it's sufficient. If it isn't, or if you're self-employed, individual disability policies are available through private insurers and are worth the cost of investigation.

Life insurance becomes relevant when other people depend on your income. If you are young, single, and without dependents, life insurance may not be an immediate priority. But if you have a partner who relies on your income, children, or family members who would face financial hardship without you, life insurance is not optional - it is a responsibility. The most straightforward option for most young people is **term life insurance**, which provides coverage for a specific period - typically 10, 20, or 30 years - at a fixed premium. Term policies are significantly more affordable than whole life or universal life policies, particularly when purchased young and healthy, and they provide the core protection most people actually need without unnecessary complexity.

Renters insurance is one of the most underutilized and underappreciated forms of coverage available, largely because most people don't realize how affordable it is. If you rent your home, your landlord's insurance covers the building - not your belongings inside it. If there is a fire, a theft, or water damage, everything you own is unprotected unless you have renters insurance. Most policies cost between $15 and $30 per month and cover personal property, liability, and in many cases temporary living expenses if your unit becomes uninhabitable. For the cost of a meal out, you can protect everything you own. There is almost no scenario where this trade-off doesn't make sense.

Auto insurance is legally required in nearly every state if you own and operate a vehicle, so most people have some form of it — but many have only the legal minimum, which may not be enough to fully protect them in a serious accident. Understanding what your policy covers, what it doesn't, and where you may be underinsured is worth a periodic review, particularly if your vehicle or financial situation has changed.

A common mistake people make with insurance is treating it as an all-or-nothing decision - either comprehensive coverage across every category or nothing at all, because the full picture feels too expensive to manage. The reality is that building your protection doesn't have to happen all at once.

Start with what matters most and build from there.

For most people, the priority order looks something like this: health insurance first, because a medical crisis is both the most likely and the most financially devastating unprotected risk. Renters insurance next, because the cost is minimal and the protection is immediate. Disability insurance as your income grows and your financial obligations increase. Life insurance when others depend on you. And a periodic review of all existing coverage to make sure what you have still matches what you need.

You don't need to solve everything this week. You need to start somewhere and keep going.

If you're between 18 and 22, this is the time to build awareness before the decisions become urgent. Understand what coverage you currently have - whether through a parent's plan, a school, or an employer - and understand when that coverage ends or changes. Know what options are available to you so that when a transition happens, you're not scrambling to figure it out under pressure.

If you're between 23 and 30, protection becomes increasingly non-negotiable. Your independence is real, your financial obligations are growing, and what you've been building deserves to be protected. An unexpected medical event, an injury that prevents you from working, or a theft that wipes out your possessions shouldn't have the power to set you back years. Insurance is what ensures that it doesn't.

Think honestly about your current level of protection. If something unexpected happened tomorrow - a medical emergency, a car accident, an injury that kept you out of work for three months - how would it affect you financially? Would you be able to manage, or would it create a level of damage that takes years to recover from?

Those aren't rhetorical questions.

They're the exact questions insurance is designed to answer before life asks them for you.

Because the goal of building a stable financial life isn't just earning more and spending wisely and saving consistently - though all of those things matter enormously. The goal is also making sure that a single bad day, a single unexpected event, a single moment where life doesn't go according to plan doesn't have the power to undo everything you've worked to create.

Insurance is what stands between your financial progress and the unpredictability of life.

It is not an expense.

It is protection for everything else you're building.

And what you're building deserves to be protected.

What To Do This Week: Conduct a simple insurance audit. Write down every type of coverage you currently have, what it covers, and what it costs. Then identify your biggest unprotected risk - the area where an unexpected event would cause the most financial damage. Research one option to address that gap this week, even if you don't act on it immediately. Knowing what's available and what it costs is the first step toward making a decision - and that step costs nothing.

13

THE TRUTH ABOUT BUYING A HOME

Few financial decisions carry as much emotional weight as buying a home. It represents something deeper than a transaction - it represents arrival. Stability. The sense that you've built enough of a life to plant yourself somewhere permanently and call it yours. Society reinforces this idea constantly. Buying a home is presented as a milestone, a marker of success, a rite of passage that separates those who are building real wealth from those who are simply getting by.

And because that narrative is so pervasive, so consistently repeated, and so emotionally compelling, most people approach homeownership as something they should do - rather than something they should carefully evaluate before doing.

That distinction matters more than most people realize.

Because buying a home can absolutely be one of the strongest financial decisions you ever make. It can build equity over time, provide stability, and become a meaningful piece of your long-term wealth. But it can also become one of the most financially stressful commitments of your life if it's entered into at the wrong time, under the wrong circumstances, or without a clear understanding of everything it actually involves.

The difference between those two outcomes is not the home.

It's the preparation.

Eric was 29 when he decided he was ready. He had been working steadily for years, his income had reached a comfortable level, and the idea of continuing to rent felt increasingly like throwing money away. Buying a home felt like the logical next step - the thing responsible adults did when they had reached a certain point in their lives. Everyone around him seemed to be doing it. The pressure, though never spoken directly, was real.

So he moved forward.

He found a place he liked, got approved for a mortgage, and closed the deal. The pride he felt was genuine. He had done it - bought a home, built equity, taken the step that felt like progress.

But within the first year, the reality of what he had taken on began to settle in ways he hadn't anticipated.

The monthly mortgage payment was manageable on its own. But the mortgage was only one piece of the actual cost. Property taxes added a significant amount on top. Homeowner's insurance was required and added more. Then the water heater failed and needed replacing. Then a section of the roof required repair. Then the HVAC system needed servicing. None of these were catastrophic individually - but together, in combination with a mortgage payment, property taxes, and insurance premiums, they created a financial pressure that felt very different from the freedom he had imagined ownership would bring.

His flexibility shrank. His savings, which had been used largely for the down payment and closing costs, hadn't fully recovered. And when expenses came up - as they always do in a home - there was less room to absorb them than he expected.

He didn't regret buying the home. But he wished someone had told him, clearly and honestly, what it actually cost to own one - not just the mortgage, but everything that came with it.

This is the conversation most people don't have before they buy. They compare their potential mortgage payment to their current rent, decide the mortgage is manageable, and treat that as sufficient analysis. But a mortgage payment and the true cost of homeownership are not the same thing - not even close.

Here is what homeownership actually costs, beyond the mortgage itself.

Property taxes are an ongoing obligation that varies significantly by location but is non-negotiable regardless. In many areas, property taxes add hundreds of dollars per month to the effective cost of owning a home. They also tend to increase over time as property values rise, which means the amount you pay when you first purchase is rarely what you'll be paying a decade later.

Homeowner's insurance is required by virtually every mortgage lender and covers the structure of your home against damage from fire, storms, and other covered events. The cost varies depending on your location, the value of the home, and the coverage level — but it is a fixed, recurring expense that adds to your monthly obligation.

Maintenance and repairs are the expenses that surprise people most, because unlike a mortgage payment, they are unpredictable in their timing and variable in their cost. A general rule used by many financial professionals is to budget between 1% and 2% of your home's value annually for maintenance and repairs. On a $300,000 home, that's

$3,000 to $6,000 per year - or $250 to $500 per month - set aside for the inevitable costs of keeping a home functioning. Some years you won't need it. Other years you'll need it all and more. The point is to expect it rather than be blindsided by it.

Closing costs are the expenses associated with completing the purchase of a home, and they are substantial - typically between 2% and 5% of the purchase price. On a $300,000 home, that's $6,000 to $15,000 paid at closing, on top of the down payment. These include lender fees, title insurance, appraisal costs, attorney fees where required, and a range of other charges that vary by location and transaction. Many first-time buyers are caught off guard by closing costs, either not anticipating them at all or significantly underestimating their amount.

The down payment itself deserves careful consideration. The traditional benchmark is 20% of the purchase price, which on a $300,000 home means $60,000 saved before you buy. A 20% down payment eliminates the requirement for private mortgage insurance - commonly known as PMI - which is an additional monthly charge required by most lenders when the down payment is less than 20%. PMI protects the lender, not you, and adds cost without providing you any benefit. Programs exist that allow buyers to purchase with lower down payments - some as low as 3% to 5% - but understanding the full cost implications of doing so is essential before choosing that path.

When all of these factors are calculated together - mortgage, taxes, insurance, maintenance, and the opportunity cost of the capital tied up in your down payment - the true monthly cost of homeownership is often significantly higher than the mortgage payment alone suggests.

Beyond the financial mechanics, there is a less-discussed but equally important dimension of homeownership that deserves honest consideration: flexibility.

When you rent, your commitment is typically measured in months. When something changes - your job, your relationship, your city, your financial situation - you have options. Renting provides mobility that ownership does not.

When you own, your commitment is measured in years. Selling a home is not a simple or inexpensive process. Real estate agent commissions typically run 5% to 6% of the sale price. There are additional closing costs on the selling side. And if the market has declined since you purchased, or if you haven't owned long enough to build meaningful equity, you may find yourself in a position where selling costs more than it returns.

The general guideline used by most financial professionals is that you should plan to stay in a home for at least five years for the purchase to make financial sense - long enough to build equity, recoup your transaction costs, and allow the market to work in your favor. If there is any significant uncertainty about your career, your location, or your personal situation over the next several years, that uncertainty is worth factoring into the decision before you commit.

Homeownership is not a flexible asset. It is a committed one. And commitment, entered into without full awareness of what it requires, has a way of creating pressure rather than providing the stability it was supposed to deliver.

None of this is meant to discourage you from buying a home. It is meant to ensure that when you do, you do so from a position of genuine readiness - not from the pressure of a timeline that was never yours to begin with.

So how do you know when you're actually ready?

The answer lives in a set of honest questions.

Is your financial foundation solid? Do you have stable income, manageable debt, and a credit profile strong enough to qualify for favorable mortgage terms? Have you saved enough for a down payment without depleting your emergency fund in the process? Could you absorb an unexpected repair of several thousand dollars within the first year without creating a financial crisis?

Is your life stable enough for this level of commitment? Are you confident in your career trajectory and your location for the foreseeable future? Is your personal situation - relationships, family plans, lifestyle - settled enough to anchor yourself to a specific place for five or more years?

And perhaps most importantly - are you buying because you are genuinely prepared, or because you feel like you should be at this stage by now?

That last question is worth sitting with honestly. The timeline that most people follow when it comes to homeownership is based on cultural expectation, not financial logic. There is no universal age at which buying a home becomes the right decision. There is only the readiness of the individual in front of that decision - and readiness is built, not assumed.

If you're between 18 and 22, homeownership is likely not an immediate decision - but understanding how it works now puts you ahead of most people who don't think about it until they're in the middle of the process. Use this time to learn, to build your credit and savings, and to develop a clear picture of what genuine financial readiness looks like so that when the decision becomes relevant, you approach it with clarity rather than pressure.

If you're between 23 and 30, the question may be becoming more real. You may be feeling the pull of ownership - from within, from peers, from family, from a market that seems to be moving faster than your savings. That pull is understandable. But the right response to it is not to rush a decision of this magnitude. The right response is to evaluate your actual readiness honestly, build toward it deliberately, and move when the foundation supports the decision - not when the pressure demands it.

A home purchased at the right time, from a position of genuine financial strength, can be one of the most powerful assets you ever own. It can grow in value, build equity that compounds over decades, provide stability for your family, and become a meaningful part of your long-term wealth.

But a home purchased before that foundation is in place - bought out of pressure, out of comparison, or out of the belief that ownership itself creates stability - can do the opposite. It can stretch your finances beyond what they can comfortably support, limit your flexibility at the exact moment life asks you to be adaptable, and turn what was supposed to be a milestone into a source of ongoing stress.

The home itself is not the variable.

Your readiness is.

So build the readiness first.

Understand the full cost.

Assess your stability honestly.

And when you move forward, move forward because you are prepared - not because you feel like it's time.

Because the goal of buying a home is not to own one.

The goal is to own one in a way that actually strengthens your life. And that only happens when preparation comes before the purchase.

What To Do This Week: Calculate your true housing readiness number. Start with the price range of homes in the area you'd consider buying, then estimate the full monthly cost - mortgage payment, property taxes, insurance, and a maintenance reserve. Compare that number to what you currently pay in rent and what your overall financial picture can genuinely support. Then check your credit score and your current savings to understand how far you are from a position of real readiness. Not to pressure yourself - but to give yourself an honest map of where you are and what you're building toward.

14

RELATIONSHIPS, MARRIAGE, AND THE REAL COST OF COMMITMENT

There are decisions in life that affect a single area - your finances, your career, your living situation - and there are decisions that affect everything simultaneously. Who you choose to build a life with is the latter. It reaches into your emotional well-being, your daily environment, your financial stability, your long-term goals, and the fundamental direction your life takes. It is, in many ways, the most consequential decision most people will ever make.

And yet, most people are never taught to approach it with the same intentionality they bring to far smaller decisions.

They are taught to follow what they feel. To trust the connection. To let love lead and assume that the practical details will work themselves out over time. And while emotion is an essential part of any meaningful relationship, emotion alone - without clarity, without honest conversation, without a shared understanding of how two lives will actually function together - is not enough to build on.

What nobody tells you is this: the most common reason relationships fail is not a lack of love. It is a lack of alignment. Two people who care deeply about each other but operate from fundamentally different assumptions about money, responsibility, communication, and the future - and who never addressed those differences directly before they became points of conflict.

This chapter is not about taking the romance out of relationships. It is about adding the awareness that makes them sustainable.

James was 28 when he met someone who felt like the right person. The connection was real, the relationship developed naturally, and over time the idea of building something permanent together felt not just possible but obvious. They moved in the direction of commitment the way most people do - led primarily by how things felt, guided by the strength of what they had built emotionally, and trusting that the rest would follow.

What they hadn't done - not in any meaningful depth - was talk about the practical architecture of a shared life.

They hadn't discussed how they each thought about money. They hadn't explored what saving meant to one versus the other, or what spending freely meant, or what financial security looked like from each of their perspectives. They hadn't talked about how decisions would be made when they disagreed, or what would happen when one person's priorities conflicted with the other's. They hadn't defined what a shared financial future actually looked like - because everything felt good enough that those conversations seemed unnecessary.

For a while, they were right.

But over time, differences that had always existed began to surface in situations where they actually mattered. One person's instinct was to save, to plan ahead, to build security. The other's instinct was to live fully in the present, to spend on experiences, to avoid the feeling of restriction that came with too much structure. Neither of these orientations was wrong. But they were different - and different, when left unaddressed, has a way of becoming divisive.

What could have been understood and navigated early - with honest conversation and genuine curiosity about each other's perspectives - became something they had to work through under the pressure of real financial decisions, real disagreements, and the weight of a commitment that was already made.

That's where most relationship difficulties actually live.

Not in the dramatic moments.

In the unaddressed differences that were always there.

Marriage, at its core, is two things simultaneously: an emotional commitment and a legal, financial partnership. Most people focus almost entirely on the first and underestimate the second - until the second begins creating pressure that affects the first.

When you marry someone, you are not simply choosing a companion. You are entering into a legal agreement that combines two financial lives in ways that have real and lasting consequences. Depending on where you live, marriage affects how property is owned, how debt is treated, how income is taxed, and what happens to assets if the relationship ends. These are not romantic considerations - but they are real ones, and understanding them before you commit is not unromantic. It is responsible.

On the financial side, the areas that most commonly create conflict in marriages are also the ones most rarely discussed before them.

Spending habits and money values are often the deepest source of financial tension in a relationship. Not because one person is right and the other is wrong, but because people develop their relationship with money early in life - shaped by their upbringing, their experiences, their sense of security - and those deeply rooted patterns don't change automatically at the altar. Someone who grew up in scarcity may be driven by a need to save and build reserves. Someone who grew up in abundance may have a more relaxed relationship with spending. Neither is inherently problematic. But when those two orientations share a bank account and a set of financial goals, the difference needs to be understood and negotiated - not assumed to resolve itself.

Debt is another area where many couples discover uncomfortable surprises. When you marry someone, you are not legally responsible for debt they incurred before the marriage in most cases - but you are sharing a life with the financial reality that debt creates. If one partner carries significant student loans, credit card balances, or other obligations, that affects the household budget, the ability to save, the qualifying terms for a mortgage, and the overall financial trajectory of the partnership. Knowing what you're entering into - honestly, specifically, without judgment - is not a test of trust. It is a foundation of it.

Income disparity - when one partner earns significantly more than the other - requires honest conversation about how expenses will be shared, how financial decisions will be made, and how both people will feel respected and empowered regardless of who earns more. Without that conversation, income disparity can quietly create power imbalances that erode the partnership over time.

Financial goals and timelines need to be aligned, or at minimum understood. If one person wants to buy a home in three years and the other wants to travel the world for five, those aren't just lifestyle differences - they're financial plans that require different behaviors today. Understanding where each person wants to go, and building a shared plan that honors both, is the work of a financial partnership. It doesn't happen automatically, and it doesn't happen once. It is an ongoing conversation that needs to be revisited as circumstances change.

There is also a legal dimension to marriage that most people enter entirely unprepared for - and that lack of preparation can have significant consequences if the relationship ends.

Divorce is not something anyone plans for at the beginning of a marriage. But it is a reality for a significant number of them, and the financial consequences of divorce - division of assets, spousal support, legal fees, and the cost of separating two financially intertwined lives - can be substantial. Understanding the legal framework of marriage in your state before you enter into it is not pessimistic. It is practical.

Prenuptial agreements - commonly called prenups - are legal documents created before marriage that define how assets, debts, and finances will be handled if the marriage ends. They are often misunderstood as tools used by the wealthy to protect themselves from their partners, or as a signal of distrust. In reality, a prenuptial agreement is simply a transparent, mutually agreed-upon plan for a scenario that neither party expects but that wisdom acknowledges as possible. They can protect both parties, clarify expectations, and prevent the kind of prolonged, expensive legal disputes that divorce without financial clarity often produces.

Whether a prenuptial agreement makes sense for your situation depends on factors including what assets each person brings into the marriage, whether either party has significant debt, whether one person will be sacrificing career advancement to support the household, and what laws govern marital property in your state. The conversation about whether to create one is worth having - not because you expect the marriage to fail, but because having an honest financial conversation before committing is exactly the kind of foundation that strong marriages are built on.

Beyond the legal and financial mechanics, the foundation of any lasting partnership is communication - specifically, the willingness to have the conversations that feel uncomfortable before they become unavoidable.

Talk about money before you share it. Understand each other's financial history - not to judge it, but to know what you're building from. Discuss debt honestly. Share your financial goals and understand theirs. Talk about how decisions will be made and what happens when you disagree. Establish whether you'll combine finances fully, keep them partially separate, or maintain individual accounts alongside a shared one.

These conversations are not a threat to intimacy.

They are an investment in it.

Because the couples who navigate financial life most successfully are not the ones who never disagree about money. They are the ones who built enough trust, transparency, and shared understanding early on that disagreements can be worked through without becoming crises.

There is one more dimension of relationships worth addressing that is rarely spoken about directly: the financial impact of choosing the wrong partner.

This is not about finding someone perfect. It is about recognizing that the person you build your life with will directly affect your financial trajectory in ways that are difficult to overstate. A partner who is financially irresponsible can undermine years of your own careful building. A partner who carries hidden debt can alter your credit, your borrowing capacity, and your financial plans. A partner who is unwilling to have honest money conversations will make every financial decision harder than it needs to be.

Conversely, a partner who is financially aligned - who shares your values around saving and spending, who communicates honestly about money, who approaches financial responsibility with the same seriousness you do - multiplies your capacity to build. Two people moving in the same financial direction, with shared goals and honest communication, can accomplish far more together than either could alone.

Who you choose matters.

Not just emotionally.

Financially, practically, and structurally - it matters enormously.

If you're between 18 and 22, you are forming your understanding of what relationships look like and what you want from them. This is the time to develop your own financial identity clearly enough that you can recognize alignment - and misalignment - when you encounter it. Pay attention to how people you're close to handle money, make decisions, and take responsibility. Those patterns tell you more about long-term compatibility than almost anything else.

If you're between 23 and 30, relationships are likely becoming more serious and the stakes are becoming more real. This is the time to bring intention to the conversations most people avoid. If you're in a committed relationship, have the financial conversations - honestly, specifically, and without assuming you already know the answers. If you're considering marriage, understand what you're entering into legally and financially, not just emotionally. The strength of a commitment is not diminished by clarity. It is built on it.

The right relationship - entered into with both emotional connection and practical alignment - is one of the most powerful forces in building a stable, meaningful life. It multiplies your capacity, your resilience, and your ability to weather the inevitable challenges that life delivers.

But the wrong relationship - or the right relationship entered into without honest communication and shared understanding - can quietly dismantle everything you've worked to build.

The difference is not luck.

It is not timing.

It is the willingness to have the conversations that feel uncomfortable before they become the conflicts that feel impossible.

So take those conversations seriously.

Ask the questions that matter.

Understand who you are building with - not just emotionally, but practically.

Because commitment is not just about being together.

It is about building something together.
And what you build together will only be as strong as the foundation you were both honest enough to lay.

What To Do This Week: Whether you're currently in a relationship or not, take time this week to clarify your own financial values. Write down your answers to these three questions: What does financial security mean to me? What are my most important financial goals over the next five years? And what are my non-negotiable expectations around how money is handled in a partnership? Knowing your own answers clearly is the first step toward recognizing - and building - genuine alignment with someone else.

PART IV

MAJOR LIFE DECISIONS

15

THE PEOPLE AROUND YOU ARE SHAPING YOUR FUTURE

There is an influence operating in your life right now that most people never fully account for - one that doesn't show up on a budget, doesn't appear in a financial plan, and isn't measured by any tool designed to track your progress. It works quietly, consistently, and almost invisibly. And over time, it shapes your habits, your decisions, your standards, and your sense of what is normal more powerfully than almost anything else in your life.

It is the people you spend the most time around.

This is not a new idea. Most people have heard some version of the principle - that you become like the people closest to you, that your environment shapes you, that the company you keep matters. Most people nod at it and move on without truly reckoning with what it means in practice. Because in practice, it means something uncomfortable: that the people around you right now - the ones you eat with, talk to, spend your weekends with, vent to, and confide in — are actively influencing the direction of your life, whether you've given them permission to or not.

Not through malice. Not through intention. Simply through the slow, steady power of proximity and repetition.

Darius was 23 and firmly embedded in a social world that felt like home. He had grown up with most of these people. They shared history, loyalty, and the kind of easy comfort that comes from years of genuine connection. There was nothing wrong with them as people - they were real friends, and the relationships were real.

But as Darius began to pay closer attention, he noticed something he hadn't been willing to see before.

The patterns around him weren't moving anywhere.

Money was spent as fast as it came in, because that was simply what everyone did. Talking about saving or investing or planning felt out of place - not because anyone actively discouraged it, but because it wasn't part of the conversation. The future was discussed in vague terms, if at all. The present was what mattered, and the present was where all the energy went.

At first, Darius told himself it didn't affect him. He was his own person. He made his own decisions. But the more honest he became with himself, the more he could see that being surrounded by a particular set of patterns had made those patterns feel normal - and things that feel normal don't get questioned. They just get repeated.

He wasn't making dramatically different decisions because everything around him reinforced the idea that his current decisions were fine.

That realization changed things.

Not overnight. Not dramatically. He didn't end friendships or walk away from people he genuinely cared about. But he began paying attention in a way he hadn't before - to what he was absorbing, to what he was accepting without examination, and to whether the direction his environment was pulling him aligned with the direction he actually wanted to go.

And slowly, intentionally, he began to seek out different conversations. Different perspectives. People who were asking different questions and making different moves. Not because his old friends were wrong, but because the version of himself he wanted to become needed different inputs than the ones he had been receiving.

Over time, his decisions changed - not because he forced them to, but because his surroundings began supporting a different direction.

That is how influence actually works.

The reason environmental influence is so powerful - and so underestimated - is that it operates beneath the level of conscious decision-making. You don't sit down and decide to adopt the financial habits of your social group. You absorb them gradually, through repetition, through observation, through the slow accumulation of what feels normal. And once something feels normal, it stops requiring justification. It just becomes what you do.

This works in both directions with equal force.

If the people around you spend freely, carry debt without concern, and treat financial planning as something for a different stage of life - that becomes the ambient standard. Deviating from it requires active, conscious effort. Maintaining it requires nothing at all.

If the people around you save consistently, talk about money with intention, invest regularly, and treat their financial future as something worth taking seriously - that becomes the ambient standard instead. The behaviors that build a strong financial life stop feeling exceptional and start feeling ordinary. And ordinary things are easy to maintain.

You don't have to be disciplined about doing what feels normal.

You just do it.

This is why your environment is not a passive backdrop to your financial life. It is an active ingredient in it.

Understanding this doesn't require you to judge the people around you, to feel superior to them, or to treat your relationships as purely transactional assessments of whether someone is helping or hindering your progress. Human relationships are far more complex and valuable than that framework allows for.

What it does require is honest awareness.

You can care deeply about someone and still recognize that their path is different from yours. You can maintain real friendships while also being intentional about where you invest your time and energy. You can appreciate what a relationship gives you emotionally while also being clear-eyed about what it reinforces in you behaviorally.

The goal is not to curate a social circle based entirely on net worth and productivity metrics. The goal is to ensure that your environment, taken as a whole, is not working against the life you are trying to build.

That might mean spending less time in situations that consistently pull you toward habits you're trying to change. It might mean actively seeking out people who are doing things you want to learn - attending events, joining communities, finding mentors, or simply starting different kinds of conversations with people already in your life. It might mean being the person in your current circle who starts asking different questions and talking about different things - because sometimes, you become the influence rather than simply being influenced.

There is also something worth naming that most conversations about environmental influence skip over: the specific impact of financial peer pressure.

It is rarely explicit. Nobody hands you a bill and tells you to spend. But the social dynamics around spending - going out when you can't afford it because everyone else is, buying things to maintain an appearance of keeping up, staying silent about financial struggles because the group norm is to project abundance - are real, and they cost real money.

Learning to navigate these dynamics without damaging your relationships or your finances requires a particular kind of confidence. The confidence to decline without elaborate explanation. The confidence to be honest about your priorities without apologizing for them. The confidence to let your choices speak for themselves rather than defending them against the unspoken pressure of what everyone else is doing.

That confidence is built over time, but it starts with clarity - clarity about what you value, where you are going, and why the short-term discomfort of occasionally moving differently than the group is worth the long-term benefit of building something real.

Beyond your social circle, there are other forms of environmental influence worth being intentional about.

The content you consume regularly shapes how you think about money, success, lifestyle, and possibility. Social media, in particular, creates a curated reality in which everyone appears to be living at a level of abundance that generates constant, low-grade pressure to keep up. The cars, the vacations, the outfits, the restaurants - most of it represents a highlight reel, not a financial reality. Consuming it uncritically and letting it define your standard of normal is one of the quietest and most expensive mistakes you can make.

The voices you listen to - the podcasts, the books, the people you follow, the conversations you seek out - shape your mental framework around what's possible and what's expected. If those voices consistently reinforce short-term thinking, consumption, and the performance of success rather than the building of it, they are working against you regardless of how entertaining they are.

Being intentional about your information environment is just as important as being intentional about your social one.

If you're between 18 and 22, this is a critical window for environmental awareness. You are forming the habits, perspectives, and definitions of normal that will carry forward into every stage of your adult life. What feels normal to you right now is being built by what surrounds you right now. That is worth taking seriously - not with anxiety, but with intentionality. Seek out environments, communities, and voices that reflect the direction you want to move, and begin reducing your exposure to the ones that consistently pull in the opposite direction.

If you're between 23 and 30, you may already be noticing the divergence - the ways in which you and people you grew up with are beginning to move in different directions, building different kinds of lives, making different kinds of choices. This divergence is natural and does not require anyone to be the villain. What it requires is honesty about which environment is supporting your growth and which is making it harder - and the willingness to make adjustments accordingly, even when those adjustments are uncomfortable.

Take an honest look at your current environment - not just the people, but the conversations, the content, the standards, and the definitions of normal that surround you daily.

Are those things moving you toward the life you want to build - or are they reinforcing patterns that you know aren't serving you?

Are you the product of your environment by default - or are you shaping your environment with intention?

Because here is what is true regardless of how motivated you are, how disciplined you are, or how clearly you can see where you want to go:

You will be influenced by what surrounds you.

The only question is whether you choose what surrounds you - or leave that choice to chance.

Choose carefully.
Not based on comfort.
Not based on history.
Not based on who is easiest to be around.
Based on direction.
Because over time, what surrounds you becomes part of you.
And what becomes part of you determines where you end up.

What To Do This Week: Spend fifteen minutes this week doing an honest environmental audit. List the five people you spend the most time with and ask yourself, genuinely, whether each relationship is reinforcing the habits and direction you want for your life - or pulling against them. Then list three sources of content you consume regularly - social media accounts, podcasts, shows - and ask the same question. You don't have to act on everything you find. But seeing it clearly is the beginning of being able to shape it intentionally.

16

LIFESTYLE CREEP - THE TRAP THAT FEELS LIKE PROGRESS

There is a financial trap that almost nobody sees coming - not because it's hidden, but because it looks exactly like success when it arrives. It doesn't feel like a mistake. It doesn't create immediate pressure or obvious warning signs. In fact, it feels like the natural, deserved reward for working hard and earning more. It feels like progress.

That feeling is precisely what makes it so dangerous.

The trap is called lifestyle creep - the gradual, almost imperceptible expansion of your spending to match every increase in your income. It happens when a raise becomes a better apartment. When a bonus becomes a newer car. When a promotion becomes dinners at nicer restaurants, better clothes, more subscriptions, more of everything. Each individual upgrade feels reasonable. Each one feels earned. And taken one at a time, each one is easy to justify.

But taken together, over time, they produce a result that nobody intended: you earn significantly more than you did before, and you have nothing more to show for it. Your lifestyle is bigger. Your expenses are higher. Your obligations have expanded. But your savings haven't grown, your investments haven't increased, and your financial position isn't meaningfully stronger than it was before the income went up.

You're just running the same race at a higher speed.

Derek received a raise at 25 that genuinely changed his monthly numbers. It wasn't life-changing money, but it was enough to create breathing room he hadn't had before - and breathing room, after a period of feeling financially tight, felt wonderful. He deserved to enjoy it. He had worked for it. So he made some adjustments.

He moved into a better apartment. Not extravagant - just nicer. He upgraded his car. Not dramatically - just newer. He allowed himself to spend more freely on food, on going out, on the small daily purchases that add texture to life. None of it felt excessive. It felt like what people do when they're doing better.

For a while, everything felt balanced.

His income had increased, his lifestyle had adjusted to match it, and nothing felt out of control. What he didn't notice - because it happened gradually, without a single defining moment - was that the breathing room he thought he had created had already been filled. The extra money that once felt like margin had been converted into obligations. The flexibility he thought he had gained had been spent before he had a chance to use it.

Then something changed at work - not dramatically, but enough to affect his income slightly. And suddenly, what had felt comfortable became tight almost immediately. Not because the change was large, but because there was no cushion. His expenses had grown to consume everything he earned, and the structure he had built required every dollar to stay in place.

He hadn't just upgraded his lifestyle.

He had upgraded his dependence.

That's the part nobody talks about when they talk about earning more. The upgrade is visible. The increased vulnerability is not. It hides inside the feeling of progress until something disrupts the pattern and makes it impossible to ignore.

Lifestyle creep is so effective at avoiding detection because it happens incrementally. No single decision feels like the problem. Upgrading your apartment when your income increases feels rational - you can afford it. Buying a newer car when your old one is aging feels reasonable - you've earned it. Spending more on experiences feels justified - you work hard and life is short.

The problem isn't any one of these decisions in isolation.

The problem is the cumulative pattern they create when they all move in the same direction at the same time - upward, always upward, always expanding to fill whatever space the income creates.

What gets lost in that pattern is the one behavior that actually changes your financial trajectory over time: the deliberate decision to let some of what you earn accumulate rather than converting all of it into a higher standard of living.

Because here is the math that lifestyle creep obscures: a dollar saved and invested is worth far more over time than a dollar spent on a lifestyle upgrade. A dollar spent on a lifestyle upgrade is gone. A dollar saved begins compounding immediately and becomes something larger over time. When every income increase gets converted entirely into spending, you are continuously choosing the dollar that disappears over the dollar that grows.

Most people make that choice without realizing they're making it - because lifestyle creep doesn't ask for your permission. It simply fills the available space.

The correction is not about deprivation. It is not about refusing to enjoy the results of your hard work or living like you're still earning your starting salary when you've long since surpassed it.

The goal is not restriction.
The goal is intentionality.

And the key to intentionality is deciding how income increases will be used before they arrive - not after, when the money is already in your account and the temptation to spend it is at its strongest.

A practical framework that many people find effective is what's sometimes called the **split rule**: when your income increases, commit in advance to directing a specific portion of that increase toward saving and investing before adjusting your lifestyle. For example, if you receive a raise that adds $400 per month to your income, you might decide that $200 goes directly to savings or investments and $200 is available to improve your lifestyle. Your standard of living improves - but your financial position improves alongside it, rather than staying flat while your expenses climb.

The exact split matters less than the principle behind it: **not every dollar of new income belongs to your lifestyle.** Some of it belongs to your future. Deciding that in advance - before you've mentally allocated it to a new expense - is the move that separates people who earn more and build more from people who earn more and simply spend more.

There is also a subtler version of lifestyle creep worth naming - one that operates not through major upgrades but through the accumulation of small, recurring expenses that individually feel inconsequential.

A new streaming subscription. A premium version of an app. A gym membership that felt cheap when you signed up. A higher-tier phone plan. Delivery fees that became a habit. Monthly boxes that seemed like a deal. Weekly purchases that became part of the routine.

None of these are significant on their own. But subscriptions and recurring expenses share a particular quality that makes them especially susceptible to accumulation without awareness: they are automatic. They charge whether you think about them or not. They continue whether you use them or not. And because they don't require a repeated decision - only the original one - they tend to multiply quietly until the total becomes something that would have given you pause if you had been asked to approve it all at once.

A periodic audit of your recurring expenses is one of the most financially effective habits you can build. Going through your bank and credit card statements to identify every recurring charge - and then honestly evaluating whether each one is still earning its place in your budget - often reveals money that has been leaving your account without your active awareness. Canceling or downgrading what you don't genuinely use is not sacrifice. It is reclaiming resources that were already yours.

Lifestyle creep also has a social dimension that is worth understanding directly.

Some of the most powerful pressure to upgrade your lifestyle doesn't come from within - it comes from the people around you. When your income increases and your social circle begins to notice, the implicit pressure to match a certain standard can be significant. Going to nicer places, buying certain things, participating in experiences at a certain price level - these can feel like the cost of belonging rather than choices you're making freely.

This connects directly to the previous chapter on environmental influence. The lifestyle standards of the people around you exert real pressure on how you spend - and if those standards are rising faster than your financial foundation can support, keeping pace with them is a form of lifestyle creep with an added social dimension.

Being clear about your own financial priorities - not as a statement to make to others, but as an internal anchor you return to when external pressure builds - is what allows you to make choices based on your actual values rather than on the performance of a lifestyle you haven't actually built yet.

If you're between 18 and 22, this is where your financial habits and identity are being formed. You may not be earning large amounts yet, but the way you relate to income increases - however small - establishes patterns that will carry forward as the numbers grow. If you learn now to save a portion of every income increase before adjusting your lifestyle, that habit will serve you powerfully for the rest of your earning life. If you learn instead to consume every increase immediately, that pattern will follow you at every income level and make building wealth consistently difficult regardless of how much you eventually earn.

If you're between 23 and 30, your income is likely growing and the temptations of lifestyle creep are becoming more real and more expensive. This is the time to be genuinely intentional. Not restrictive - intentional. Give yourself permission to enjoy your progress. And simultaneously, give your future self the gift of a financial foundation that grows alongside your lifestyle, not one that gets left behind every time your spending expands.

Take an honest look at your last two or three income increases - raises, bonuses, side income that grew, or any other moment when more money became available to you. What happened to that additional income? Did your savings grow? Did your investments increase? Or did your spending simply expand to absorb it, leaving your financial position essentially unchanged at a higher cost level?

There is no judgment in those questions.

There is only information.

And information, looked at honestly, tells you everything you need to know about the pattern you've been running - and whether it's the pattern you actually want to continue.

Because lifestyle creep doesn't care about your intentions.

It responds to your habits.

And habits, once you can see them clearly, can be changed.
Not dramatically.
Not all at once.

But deliberately, incrementally, and with the understanding that every dollar you redirect from lifestyle expansion toward financial foundation is a dollar that begins working for your future rather than simply maintaining your present.

That redirection - small, consistent, intentional - is the difference between earning more and actually building more.
And building more is the whole point.

What To Do This Week: Pull up your bank and credit card statements from the past three months and identify every recurring charge - subscriptions, memberships, automatic renewals, and regular services. Write down the total. Then go through each one and mark it as either actively used and worth the cost, rarely used and worth reconsidering, or forgotten entirely and worth canceling immediately. Then ask yourself: the last time your income increased, where did that additional money go? If you can't answer that clearly, that's your starting point.

17

EMERGENCY FUNDS - YOUR FIRST LINE OF DEFENSE

If there is one financial tool that consistently separates people who handle unexpected situations with relative calm from people who are sent into immediate crisis by them, it is not a high income, a strong credit score, or a sophisticated investment strategy.

It is a pile of cash sitting in a savings account doing nothing exciting whatsoever.

It is an emergency fund - and despite how unglamorous it sounds, despite the fact that it generates minimal returns and requires you to leave money sitting untouched for months or years at a time, it may be the single most stabilizing financial decision you can make right now.

Here is why: life is unpredictable in ways that are entirely predictable. Not in the sense that you can foresee exactly what will go wrong, but in the sense that something always does. A car breaks down. A medical bill appears. A job situation changes. A home repair cannot be postponed. A flight has to be booked on short notice for a family emergency. These are not rare events reserved for people with particularly bad luck. They are the normal texture of adult life - the expected unexpected, arriving on a timeline that never aligns with your convenience.

The question is never whether something will come up.

The question is whether you will be able to handle it without dismantling everything else you've been building.

Tasha was 26 and finally hitting a financial stride that felt sustainable. Steady income, manageable bills, a routine she could live within comfortably. Things weren't perfect, but they felt stable - and stable, after a period of instability, felt like enough. She wasn't saving much beyond her basic expenses, but nothing had gone wrong yet, and nothing going wrong felt like permission to relax.

Then her car needed a major repair.

Not a minor inconvenience - a significant failure that made the car undrivable and, given that she needed it to get to work, non-negotiable to fix. The cost was more than she had available. Not dramatically more. Just more than what was sitting in her account when the bill arrived.

So she did what most people in that situation do.

She put it on a credit card.

The problem was solved. The car was fixed. Life resumed its normal pace. But what had been a one-time expense became a recurring obligation - monthly payments, interest accumulating in the background, a portion of her income committed every month to a repair that had already been made and was long since forgotten. What could have been a temporary disruption became a persistent drag on her finances that followed her for months.

Not because the repair was catastrophic.

Because there was nothing in place to absorb it.

That's the role of an emergency fund - not to prevent unexpected expenses from occurring, but to prevent them from cascading. To absorb the shock so that one bad week doesn't become six months of financial recovery. To give you the ability to respond to life's inevitable surprises without reaching for debt as the only available option.

Most people understand the concept of an emergency fund intellectually. What stops them from building one is a combination of competing priorities, the sense that the amount required is too large to achieve quickly, and the quiet belief that things will probably be fine without one - a belief that tends to hold right up until it doesn't.

The most important thing to understand about building an emergency fund is that the size of it is far less important than the existence of it.

Starting with a goal of $500 is not inadequate. It is a beginning - and a beginning that already changes your ability to handle a flat tire, an unexpected copay, or a short gap in income without immediately turning to credit. Once that first $500 is in place, the goal shifts to $1,000. Then to one month of essential expenses. Then to two. Then, over time, to the fully established benchmark that most financial professionals recommend: three to six months of essential living expenses held in a liquid, accessible savings account.

That final number can feel intimidating when you're starting from zero. It is not meant to be reached in a month. It is meant to be built gradually, consistently, and with the understanding that every dollar added to it is a dollar of insulation between you and the next unexpected situation - however large or small that situation turns out to be.

The path from nothing to fully funded is built one consistent contribution at a time.

There are a few principles that make building an emergency fund significantly more effective than simply hoping to save whatever is left over at the end of each month.

Keep it separate. Your emergency fund should live in a dedicated savings account that is not connected to your everyday checking account in a way that makes it easy to dip into. Out of sight is not entirely out of mind, but it reduces the temptation to treat your emergency fund as a secondary spending account for purchases that feel urgent but aren't actually emergencies. A high-yield savings account - which offers a higher interest rate than a traditional savings account while keeping your money fully liquid and accessible - is an excellent vehicle for this purpose. Your money grows modestly while it waits, and it remains available when you actually need it.

Define what counts as an emergency. This sounds obvious, but it matters. An emergency fund exists for genuine, unexpected, necessary expenses - a medical situation, a car repair that affects your ability to work, a sudden loss of income, a home repair that cannot be safely postponed. It does not exist for a sale you don't want to miss, a vacation that came up last minute, or a purchase you've been wanting to make but haven't budgeted for. Keeping those boundaries clear protects the fund from gradual erosion by expenses that feel urgent in the moment but are not what the fund was built for.

Automate the contribution. As with every other savings goal, the most effective approach is to remove the monthly decision from the equation entirely. Set up an automatic transfer that moves a fixed amount into your emergency fund on the same day every pay period. Treat it as a non-negotiable expense rather than an optional contribution. Over time, this becomes part of your financial infrastructure -

something that happens in the background without requiring ongoing effort or discipline to maintain.

Rebuild it when you use it. This is the step most people forget, or delay longer than they should. When your emergency fund gets used for an actual emergency - which is exactly what it's there for - the priority immediately after resolving the situation is to rebuild it. An emergency fund that has been depleted and not replenished is no longer doing its job. Make rebuilding it the first financial priority after the crisis passes, before lifestyle expenses expand to absorb the income that had been going toward the fund.

There is a psychological dimension to having an emergency fund that is difficult to quantify but impossible to overstate once you've experienced it.

When you know that a certain amount of money is sitting in reserve - money that exists specifically to handle the unexpected - the low-grade financial anxiety that most people carry quietly in the background begins to ease. Not disappear entirely, because financial life always involves some uncertainty. But ease. The sense of being one bad week away from a crisis - a feeling so common that most people accept it as a normal part of adult life - begins to recede.

That shift in how you move through your daily life is real and valuable. It affects how you make decisions. It affects how you handle stress. It affects your willingness to take considered risks in other areas of your life, because you know that a safety net exists if something doesn't go as planned. It changes the texture of your relationship with money from one of constant vigilance and managed anxiety to one of earned confidence.

That confidence is not arrogance. It is not the belief that nothing can go wrong.

It is the knowledge that if something does, you are prepared for it. And that knowledge changes everything about how you show up for the rest of your financial life.

There is also a practical interaction between your emergency fund and your other financial goals that is worth understanding clearly. Without an emergency fund, every unexpected expense becomes a threat to your other financial progress. An unexpected car repair gets put on a credit card, which increases your debt load and costs you interest over time. An unexpected medical bill depletes savings that were earmarked for something else. A short period of reduced income forces you to pause investment contributions or miss bill payments. Each disruption sets back progress that took months to build.

With an emergency fund in place, unexpected expenses are absorbed by the fund - which is exactly what it was designed to do - and your other financial structures remain intact. Your credit card balance doesn't increase. Your investments continue uninterrupted. Your monthly obligations stay manageable. The disruption is real, but it is contained rather than cascading.

This is the financial concept of insulation in its most practical form. Your emergency fund is the barrier between life's unpredictability and the financial foundation you've been building. Without it, every unexpected event has a direct line to your most important financial goals. With it, that line is broken.

That protection is worth prioritizing early - even before investing, even before accelerating debt repayment beyond minimum payments - because without it, every other financial goal is more vulnerable than it needs to be.

If you're between 18 and 22, building even a small emergency fund right now - before your expenses are significant and before life has handed you the full complexity it eventually will - is one of the highest-value financial moves available to you. Start with a goal of $500. Then $1,000. You don't need to get there in a month. You need to get there before you need it - and you never know when that will be.

If you're between 23 and 30, the stakes around an emergency fund are becoming more real with every passing year. Your expenses are larger. Your obligations are more significant. The financial impact of an unexpected disruption is greater than it was a few years ago - and it will only continue to grow as your life does. If you don't have an emergency fund in place, this is the area to prioritize before almost anything else. Not because it's the most exciting financial goal, but because it is the one that protects every other goal you're working toward.

Think honestly about where you are right now.

If your car broke down tomorrow and the repair cost $1,200, how would you handle it? If you had a medical expense of $800 next month that insurance didn't cover, where would that money come from? If your income was reduced or interrupted for thirty days, how long could you sustain your current obligations before something started to crack?

These aren't hypothetical questions designed to frighten you.

They are the questions your life will eventually ask - in its own timing, on its own terms, without regard for whether you're ready.

The emergency fund is your answer to those questions before they're asked.

It is the financial equivalent of carrying an umbrella not because you're certain it will rain, but because you know weather is unpredictable and being caught in a downpour without one is entirely avoidable.

So build it.

Start small if you have to.
Automate it.
Protect it.
Rebuild it when it gets used.

Because the months when nothing goes wrong, the emergency fund will sit quietly in its account doing very little.

And the one month when everything goes wrong at once - it will be the most important money you have.

What To Do This Week: Open a dedicated high-yield savings account specifically for your emergency fund if you don't already have one. Search for "best high-yield savings accounts" to find current options - rates change frequently, so real-time research will serve you better than any specific recommendation here. Then set up an automatic transfer - whatever amount is realistic for your current situation, even if it's $25 or $50 per pay period - to move into that account on the same day you get paid. Name the account "Emergency Fund" so it carries its purpose visually every time you see it. Then leave it alone until you actually need it.

18

DEBT - THE WEIGHT YOU DON'T FEEL RIGHT AWAY

Debt is one of the few financial forces that can feel like help right up until the moment it becomes a burden. It arrives offering solutions. It fills gaps, creates access, and makes possible things that wouldn't be possible otherwise. In the beginning, it asks very little in return. The payments are manageable. The balance seems controllable. The decision to use it feels not just reasonable but smart - a practical tool applied to a real problem.

That is the nature of debt at its most deceptive.

Because debt doesn't reveal its true weight immediately. It builds it. Quietly, incrementally, through decisions that each make individual sense but collectively create something heavier than any of them suggested on their own. And by the time the weight becomes undeniable - by the time the monthly obligations are consuming a portion of your income that genuinely limits your choices - the debt is no longer new. It is established. It has history. And the work required to address it is significantly greater than the awareness required to have prevented it.

Chris was 24 when he started reaching for credit as a regular part of managing his life. Not dramatically. Not irresponsibly. Just practically - the way most people do when they're building something and the resources don't always match the requirements.
A new phone when his old one stopped working reliably. Furniture for his apartment that he needed now and planned to pay off over time. A few unexpected expenses that arrived before the paycheck that would have covered them. Each decision made sense in the moment. Each balance felt manageable in isolation. Nothing about any individual choice raised a flag.

But over time, the individual choices became a collective reality. One balance became several. One monthly payment became multiple. What had once felt like occasional, controlled use of credit had gradually become a structural feature of his monthly finances - a fixed portion of every paycheck already committed before he had a chance to direct it anywhere else. His flexibility shrank in direct proportion to the obligations that had accumulated. And what had entered his life as a series of solutions had quietly become a constraint.

He hadn't planned to carry debt. He had simply used credit the way most people do - as a tool for managing the present - without fully accounting for the way those decisions stack up over time into something that begins managing him.

That's the trajectory most debt follows.

Not a dramatic fall. A gradual accumulation. And a slow, dawning recognition that the weight you're carrying is heavier than the individual pieces suggested it would be.

To understand debt clearly, it helps to separate it into two fundamentally different categories - because not all debt works the same way, and not all debt deserves the same response.

The first category is **intentional debt** - borrowed money applied to something with a clear, considered purpose. A mortgage on a home that fits your financial readiness and your long-term plan. A student loan for education that leads to a career with meaningful earning potential. A business loan to fund something with a realistic path to return. Intentional debt is not inherently problematic. It is a financial tool - one that, used with clarity and discipline, can enable outcomes that would otherwise be out of reach.

What makes debt intentional is not the category it falls into, but the thinking behind it. Intentional debt answers three questions before the borrowing happens: What is this money for? What is the full cost - not just the monthly payment, but the total amount paid including interest over the life of the loan? And how will this be repaid, specifically, within a timeframe that doesn't compromise other financial priorities?

When those questions can be answered clearly and honestly, borrowing can be a legitimate and effective financial move.

The second category is **reactive debt** - borrowed money used to fill gaps, manage shortfalls, maintain a lifestyle, or handle situations that weren't prepared for. Credit card balances that carry from month to month. Personal loans taken to cover expenses that income couldn't support. Debt used not to build something, but to sustain something that the current financial structure can't actually afford.

Reactive debt is where most financial damage accumulates. Not because any single instance is catastrophic, but because the pattern - borrowing to fill gaps, paying minimums, and borrowing again when the next gap appears - creates a cycle that is expensive to maintain and difficult to exit. Interest compounds on balances that never fully resolve. Monthly minimums preserve the debt without reducing it meaningfully. And the financial flexibility that might otherwise be used to build something gets consumed by the cost of managing what already exists.

Most people who carry significant debt didn't set out to be in debt. They set out to handle situations as they came up - and credit was the tool that made that possible. The debt was the accumulation of those moments, not a plan anyone consciously made.

Interest is the mechanism that transforms manageable debt into significant debt, and it deserves to be understood clearly - because most people interact with it without truly grasping what it does over time.

Interest is the cost of borrowing. It is expressed as an annual percentage rate - APR - and it compounds, meaning it is calculated not just on the original amount borrowed but on the balance including previously accumulated interest. This compounding effect is the reason that minimum payments on a high-interest balance can feel like they're making progress while actually changing the balance very little.

Here is a concrete illustration of what this means in practice. If you carry a $3,000 balance on a credit card with a 24% APR - which is not an uncommon rate - and you make only the minimum payment each month, it will take you well over a decade to pay off that balance, and you will pay more than double the original amount by the time it's resolved. The purchase that felt like $3,000 at the time of swipe will have cost significantly more by the time the debt is retired.

This is not a hypothetical designed to create alarm. It is the mathematical reality of how high-interest revolving debt works - and understanding it changes how you relate to every credit card balance you carry.

The goal is not to be afraid of credit. It is to be clear-eyed about its cost, so that decisions about carrying balances are made with full awareness rather than the comfortable assumption that minimum payments are a sufficient strategy.

If you currently carry debt, the path forward begins with clarity - not judgment, not panic, but a clear and honest accounting of exactly where you stand.

This means knowing, specifically, what you owe. Not approximately. Not in rough categories. Specifically - every account, every balance, every interest rate, every minimum payment. Most people have a general sense of their debt without having a precise picture of it. That vagueness is not neutral. It is a form of avoidance that makes it harder to address what exists and easier to accumulate more.

Once you have a clear picture, the next step is creating a repayment strategy. There are two primary approaches most financial professionals recommend, and the right one depends on your psychology and your specific debt profile.

The **avalanche method** directs extra repayment toward the debt with the highest interest rate first, while maintaining minimum payments on all others. When the highest-rate debt is eliminated, you redirect that payment toward the next highest, and so on. Mathematically, this is the most efficient approach - it minimizes the total interest paid over the life of your debt and gets you to zero fastest.

The **snowball method** directs extra repayment toward the smallest balance first, regardless of interest rate. When that balance is eliminated, you redirect its payment toward the next smallest. This approach costs more in interest over time, but it creates early wins - moments where a debt is fully eliminated - that provide psychological momentum and motivation to continue. For people who have struggled with consistency in debt repayment, the emotional traction of early victories can be worth the additional interest cost.

Neither method works without one essential element: making more than the minimum payment. Minimum payments are designed to keep debt alive for as long as possible. They generate maximum interest income for the lender. Paying more than the minimum - even modestly more - compresses the timeline significantly and reduces the total cost substantially. Whatever extra you can direct toward repayment, directed consistently, accelerates your exit from the cycle.

While paying down existing debt, it is equally important to stop adding to it.

This sounds obvious, but it is harder in practice than it appears — particularly if debt has become a habitual tool for managing monthly shortfalls. If you are regularly spending more than your income supports and filling the gap with credit, no repayment strategy will resolve the situation, because the debt being paid down is being rebuilt as fast as it's being eliminated.

The solution to this pattern is not simply willpower. It is structural. It requires an honest look at the gap between income and spending, and a genuine effort to close that gap - either by reducing spending, increasing income, or both. Until the inflow and outflow are in balance, debt reduction is a holding pattern rather than a genuine exit.

This is also why emergency funds and debt reduction are not competing priorities - they work together. A modest emergency fund, even one as small as $500 to $1,000, prevents the cycle where unexpected expenses get charged to credit and immediately rebuild balances that were just paid down. Without that cushion, a single car repair or medical bill can undo months of debt repayment progress in a single transaction.

There are also situations where debt has moved beyond the realm of self-managed repayment - where the balances are significant enough, the interest rates high enough, or the monthly obligations overwhelming enough that a different kind of intervention may be warranted.

In these cases, several options exist that are worth understanding. **Balance transfer cards** allow you to move high-interest credit card debt to a new card with a low or zero introductory interest rate for a defined promotional period - typically 12 to 21 months. This can create a window in which your payments reduce the principal directly rather than being consumed by interest. The key discipline required is paying off the balance before the promotional period ends, after which the rate typically reverts to a high standard APR.

Debt consolidation loans combine multiple debts into a single loan with one monthly payment, often at a lower interest rate than the combined rates of the debts being consolidated. This simplifies repayment and can reduce the monthly cost, but it only helps if the spending patterns that created the debt in the first place have also been addressed - otherwise, consolidation simply frees up the original credit accounts to accumulate new balances.

Nonprofit credit counseling agencies offer free or low-cost debt management support, including negotiating with creditors on your behalf and creating structured repayment plans. The National Foundation for Credit Counseling - NFCC - is a reputable resource for finding accredited nonprofit credit counselors. This option can be valuable for people whose debt load feels genuinely unmanageable and who need structured support to navigate it.

What to avoid: predatory debt settlement companies that promise to eliminate debt for a fraction of what you owe, typically in exchange for upfront fees and with significant risks to your credit. The results are rarely as advertised, and the damage to your credit and finances in the process can be substantial.

If you're between 18 and 22, this is your opportunity to build the understanding that prevents reactive debt from becoming a feature of your financial life. You don't need to experience debt extensively to learn from it. The patterns that create it are predictable - spending beyond income, using credit as a substitute for saving, and treating minimum payments as a sufficient repayment strategy. Knowing those patterns now means you can avoid them before they establish themselves.

If you're between 23 and 30, you may already be managing some level of debt. The goal now is not to feel behind - it is to see clearly and act deliberately. Know what you owe. Create a repayment strategy. Stop adding to the balance while you work to reduce it. And build the emergency fund that prevents the cycle from rebuilding itself every time something unexpected happens.

Take an honest inventory of where you stand with debt right now.
Not a general sense. A specific one.

Write down every balance you carry, every interest rate attached to it, and every minimum payment required. Add them up. Look at the total clearly. Then ask yourself: if nothing about your current behavior changed, how long would this debt follow you? What is it costing you in interest per month? What could you be doing with that money if it weren't committed to repaying the past?

These questions are not meant to create shame.
They are meant to create clarity.

Because debt, seen clearly, becomes something you can address.
Avoided, it becomes something that grows while you look away.

The weight of debt is real.
But it is not permanent.

It is reducible - through consistent action, a clear strategy, and the discipline to stop adding to what you're working to eliminate.

Every payment above the minimum shortens the timeline.
Every month without a new balance is progress.
Every dollar redirected from debt service toward saving and building represents a piece of your financial life reclaimed.

The weight lifts gradually.

But it lifts.

And on the other side of it is something worth working toward:

Income that is yours to direct.
Flexibility that isn't already committed.
A financial life that is building forward -
instead of one that is still paying for the past.

What To Do This Week: Write down every debt you currently carry - credit cards, personal loans, student loans, car payments, anything. For each one, note the current balance, the interest rate, and the minimum monthly payment. Then calculate the total. If you've been avoiding this exercise, that avoidance is itself information worth paying attention to. Once you have the complete picture in front of you, identify the one debt you will focus on first — either the highest interest rate or the smallest balance, depending on which approach resonates more - and calculate what an extra $25, $50, or $100 per month directed toward that balance would do to the payoff timeline. Seeing the math is often the most motivating thing you can do.

19

STUDENT LOANS - THE DEBT YOU SIGNED FOR BEFORE YOU UNDERSTOOD IT

There is a particular kind of debt that is unique in almost every way that matters. It is taken on by people who are, in many cases, still teenagers. It is signed for before the borrower has any real sense of what their future income will look like, what the monthly payments will actually feel like against a real budget, or what it means to carry a five or six figure obligation into the first decade of their adult life. It is often described as an investment - in yourself, in your future, in your earning potential - in a way that makes the decision feel not just acceptable but responsible.

And yet, for millions of people, student loan debt becomes one of the heaviest and most persistent financial burdens they carry - not because education isn't valuable, but because the borrowing decisions that funded it were made without the understanding that the weight of those decisions deserved.

This chapter is not an argument against education or against borrowing to fund it when necessary. It is an argument for understanding what you are signing before you sign it, managing what you already owe as effectively as possible, and making future education decisions with clear eyes rather than the assumption that the debt will somehow take care of itself.

Jordan was 18 when she signed her first student loan documents. She was excited about school, focused on getting in, and not particularly focused on the numbers attached to the financial aid package. The loan amounts felt abstract - large in theory, but distant in practice. She would deal with them after graduation, when she had a job and an income and a real financial life to manage them from.

Four years later, she graduated with a degree she was proud of and a loan balance she hadn't looked at closely since the day she signed.

When she finally sat down with the full picture - total balance, interest rates, monthly payment under the standard repayment plan - the numbers were sobering. Not impossible. But real in a way they hadn't felt when she was 18 and the money was flowing toward tuition rather than away from her paycheck.

The monthly payment under standard repayment was more than she expected. It competed directly with rent, with car payments, with the emergency fund she was trying to build, and with the retirement contributions she knew she should be making. Every dollar going toward loan repayment was a dollar not going somewhere else - and the somewhere elses were all important.
She wasn't in crisis. But she was constrained in ways she hadn't anticipated - because at 18, she hadn't been equipped to anticipate them.

That gap between signing and understanding is where most student loan difficulty begins.

Before addressing how to manage student loans, it's worth understanding the basic landscape — because student loans are not a single, uniform thing. They come in different forms, with different terms, different interest rates, and different rules governing repayment and relief.

Federal student loans are issued by the U.S. government and carry a set of protections and flexibilities that private loans do not. They come in two primary forms for undergraduate borrowers: Direct Subsidized Loans, where the government covers the interest while you are enrolled at least half-time, and Direct Unsubsidized Loans, where interest begins accumulating from the day the loan is disbursed - including during school, during grace periods, and during any deferment. Graduate students and parents may encounter Direct PLUS Loans, which carry higher interest rates and fewer income-driven repayment options.

Federal loans offer meaningful protections that make them significantly more manageable than private alternatives in most circumstances. Income-driven repayment plans, deferment and forbearance options during financial hardship, and various forgiveness programs are all features exclusive to federal loans. If you have federal loans, understanding these options is not optional knowledge - it is essential to managing your debt effectively.

Private student loans are issued by banks, credit unions, and other private lenders. They do not carry the protections of federal loans. Interest rates are typically variable rather than fixed, meaning they can increase over time. Repayment terms are set by the lender rather than governed by federal programs. Income-driven repayment plans, federal forgiveness programs, and most deferment options do not apply. Private loans are generally a last resort - appropriate only when federal loan limits have been exhausted and the remaining gap cannot be covered through other means.

If you have a mix of federal and private loans, understanding which is which - and treating them accordingly - is one of the most important first steps in managing your debt effectively.

The mechanics of student loan interest deserve specific attention, because they work in ways that surprise many borrowers who weren't focused on the details when they signed.

Interest on most student loans begins accumulating immediately upon disbursement - not at graduation, not at the end of the grace period, but from the moment the money is released. On unsubsidized federal loans and all private loans, interest accrues throughout school. If that interest is not paid during enrollment, it capitalizes - meaning it is added to the principal balance at the end of the grace period. Once capitalized, you are paying interest on the original loan amount plus all the interest that accumulated while you were in school.

This is why borrowers sometimes graduate and discover that their loan balance is already higher than the amount they originally borrowed. The loan grew while they were in school, and the growth was built into the structure from the beginning.

Understanding this before you borrow - and understanding it now if you've already borrowed - changes how you relate to the debt. It makes clear why paying even small amounts toward interest during school, if possible, can meaningfully reduce the balance you carry into repayment. And it makes clear why extending repayment timelines, while it reduces monthly payments, dramatically increases the total cost of the loan over its life.

If you currently have student loans in repayment, the most important thing you can do is understand your options - because federal student loans in particular offer more flexibility than most borrowers realize.

Standard repayment divides your balance into fixed monthly payments over ten years. It is the default plan and the one that minimizes total interest paid. If you can manage the standard payment without significant hardship, it is generally the most cost-effective path.

Income-driven repayment plans - including Income-Based Repayment, Pay As You Earn, and Saving on a Valuable Education, known as SAVE - calculate your monthly payment as a percentage of your discretionary income rather than as a fixed amount based on your balance. For borrowers whose loan payments under standard repayment would create genuine financial hardship relative to their income, these plans can provide meaningful relief. They extend the repayment timeline and increase the total interest paid, but they also cap payments at a level that your income can support and include provisions for forgiveness of any remaining balance after a defined repayment period - typically 20 to 25 years, depending on the plan.

Public Service Loan Forgiveness - commonly known as PSLF - is available to borrowers who work full-time for qualifying government or nonprofit employers and make 120 qualifying payments under an income-driven repayment plan. After those 120 payments - ten years of qualifying employment - the remaining balance is forgiven, tax-free. For borrowers in public service careers, PSLF can be one of the most powerful debt relief tools available. But it requires precise adherence to the program's requirements, and the details matter significantly. If you believe you may qualify, researching the current program requirements and certifying your employment annually from the beginning of your career is essential.

Teacher Loan Forgiveness and other profession-specific programs exist for educators, healthcare workers, military service members, and others. These programs vary in their terms and benefit amounts - researching what applies to your specific career path is worth the time investment.

To explore all federal repayment options and model the impact of different plans on your specific loan balance and income, the Federal Student Aid website - StudentAid.gov - is the authoritative resource. The Loan Simulator tool available there allows you to compare repayment plans side by side, with estimates of monthly payments and total costs under each. Using it costs nothing and can change how you approach your repayment strategy significantly.

For borrowers managing significant student loan debt, a few additional principles apply.

Know your servicer. Your loan servicer is the company responsible for managing your federal loans - processing payments, handling repayment plan changes, and communicating about your account. Your servicer may have changed since you first borrowed, and keeping your contact information current with them is essential. Missed communications from your servicer can lead to missed deadlines, lost opportunities for repayment plan adjustments, and in some cases, unnecessary default.

Don't ignore your loans. Student loans that enter default - which occurs after 270 days of missed payments on federal loans - carry serious consequences. Your entire balance becomes immediately due. Your credit score is significantly damaged. The government can garnish your wages, your tax refunds, and even Social Security benefits to recover the debt. Default is not a resolution - it is an escalation. If you are struggling to make payments, the options available to you before default are far better than anything available after it. Contact your servicer before missing a payment, not after.

Refinancing is an option that allows you to replace existing student loans - federal, private, or both - with a new private loan at a different interest rate. If your credit score and income have improved significantly since you first borrowed, refinancing may offer a lower interest rate and reduced total cost. However, refinancing federal loans into a private loan permanently eliminates access to federal protections - income-driven repayment, forgiveness programs, deferment options, and all other federal benefits. This trade-off deserves very careful consideration. Refinancing can make sense for borrowers with strong financial positions who have no intention of pursuing forgiveness and whose income is stable enough that the loss of income-driven repayment protection is not a meaningful risk. For everyone else, the flexibility of federal loans is typically worth more than the interest rate reduction refinancing might provide.

For anyone considering taking on student loans in the future - or considering additional education that would require borrowing - a few questions deserve honest answers before signing anything.
What is the realistic earning potential of the career this degree leads to, and how does that compare to the debt required to pursue it? A degree that leads to a career with a starting salary of $40,000 and a loan balance of $80,000 creates a very different financial reality than the same debt load attached to a career beginning at $75,000. The ratio matters - and it is a calculation most prospective borrowers never make before committing.

Have all non-loan options been fully explored? Scholarships, grants, employer tuition assistance, community college for foundational coursework, in-state tuition at public institutions, work-study programs — these reduce the amount that needs to be borrowed and deserve thorough investigation before loans are accepted.

Is the loan amount being considered the maximum available, or the minimum necessary? Financial aid packages often present the maximum loan amount a student is eligible to borrow. Many students borrow the full amount without evaluating whether less would cover their actual needs. Borrowing less, even if more is available, reduces the balance that enters repayment - and every dollar not borrowed is a dollar not accumulating interest.

Is this the right time for this education, or would working for a period, building savings, and then attending reduce the borrowing required? The cultural pressure to proceed directly from high school to a four-year degree on a conventional timeline leads many people to borrow more than necessary at a stage when they have the fewest resources to manage it. A different sequence - work, save, attend with reduced borrowing - is not available to everyone, but for those for whom it is, it is worth serious consideration.

If you're between 18 and 22, you may be in the middle of this decision right now - choosing schools, evaluating financial aid packages, signing loan documents. The most important thing you can do is slow down enough to understand what you are committing to. Calculate what your monthly payment will look like under standard repayment when you graduate. Compare it to a realistic starting salary in your intended field. Understand whether the debt load is proportionate to the opportunity. And borrow only what you genuinely need - not what is available.

If you're between 23 and 30, you are likely already in repayment or approaching it. The most important thing you can do is get a complete and accurate picture of what you owe, understand your repayment options, and choose the strategy that balances your monthly financial reality with the long-term goal of eliminating the debt as efficiently as possible. Log in to StudentAid.gov today if you haven't recently - know your balance, your servicer, your current repayment plan, and what other options are available to you.

Student loans are not a life sentence. They are a debt - significant, often heavy, but finite and manageable with the right approach.
The borrowers who navigate them most successfully are not the ones who earn the most or got the best interest rates. They are the ones who understood what they signed, knew their options, and made deliberate decisions about repayment rather than defaulting to whatever plan required the least immediate attention.

That understanding, applied consistently, is what turns student debt from a source of long-term financial drag into something you move through - and beyond.

The education was worth pursuing.
Make sure the debt doesn't cost more than it should.
And if you haven't looked at your loans recently —
look today.

What To Do This Week: Log in to StudentAid.gov and pull up your complete federal loan summary - total balance, interest rates, current repayment plan, and servicer information. If you have private loans, locate those statements as well. Then use the Loan Simulator on StudentAid.gov to compare your current repayment plan to at least two alternatives - including an income-driven option if your current payment feels like a strain. Write down what you find. Knowing exactly where you stand is the foundation of every good decision that follows.

PART V

MINDSET & REALITY

20

THE POWER OF CONSISTENCY OVER TIME

If you could identify the single factor that separates people who build strong financial lives from people who struggle to - the one variable that matters more than income, more than opportunity, more than intelligence or education or luck - it would not be what most people expect.

It would not be a dramatic decision. Not a windfall. Not a perfect strategy executed at exactly the right moment.

It would be something far less exciting, far less visible, and far more powerful than any of those things.

It would be consistency.

Not consistency when it's easy. Not consistency when motivation is high and the path feels clear and the results are visible. Consistency when none of those things are true - when the progress feels slow, when the results are invisible, when the easier choice is to stop and restart later. That kind of consistency - the kind that continues not because it feels rewarding but because it has been decided - is what actually builds something over time.

Most people never develop it. Not because they lack discipline or intelligence or desire, but because they misunderstand how progress actually works. They expect it to be visible. They expect it to feel significant. They expect the effort to produce results they can see in a timeframe that keeps them motivated.
And when that doesn't happen, they stop.

Maya was 22 when she made a decision that didn't feel significant at the time. She had been thinking about getting better with money - saving more, spending less, building something instead of just maintaining her current situation. She had heard the advice many times. She understood it, at least conceptually. What she hadn't done was act on it in any consistent way.

So she started small. Deliberately, almost uncomfortably small.
She set aside a fixed amount every week - modest enough that it didn't strain her budget, consistent enough that it happened regardless of how the week had gone. She didn't announce it. She didn't track it obsessively. She simply did it, week after week, as a quiet commitment she had made to herself.

In the beginning, nothing seemed different.

The amount felt too small to matter. The progress felt too slow to celebrate. There were weeks when it would have been easier to skip it - when something came up, when money felt tight, when the discipline required felt disproportionate to the results being produced.

She kept going anyway.

Months passed. Then a year. Then several.

And what had once felt insignificant had become something she could see clearly - a foundation that hadn't existed before, built entirely from small actions repeated without fanfare over a long period of time. Not through a single good decision. Not through a dramatic shift. Through the accumulation of many small ones, each unremarkable on its own, collectively remarkable in their result.

That is how consistency actually works.

It doesn't announce itself. It compounds quietly. And by the time the results become visible, the habit that created them has already become simply the way things are done.

The reason most people struggle with consistency is that they confuse it with motivation - and motivation, by its nature, is unreliable.

Motivation is the feeling that makes starting easy. It is the energy present at the beginning of a new financial plan, a new saving commitment, a new intention to handle money differently. It feels powerful in the moment, and it is - for a moment. But motivation is responsive to results, and financial results are slow. They don't arrive on a timeline that keeps motivation sustained. They arrive quietly, gradually, often imperceptibly, until suddenly they are undeniable.

The gap between when you start and when you can clearly see what you're building is where motivation fails and where most people stop. Not because they were wrong to start. Because they expected the feeling of starting to carry them further than feelings ever can.

Consistency is different from motivation in one critical way: it is not based on how you feel. It is based on what you have decided. It operates independent of energy, independent of enthusiasm, independent of whether today feels like a good day to follow through. It is the decision, made once, executed repeatedly, without requiring re-authorization every time the moment arrives.

This is why systems matter more than willpower.

Willpower is a resource that depletes. Every decision that requires active resistance draws on a pool that has limits. By the end of a long day, a difficult week, or a financially stressful period, the willpower available for good financial decisions is often genuinely diminished - not because you are weak, but because you are human.

Systems remove decisions from moments. When saving is automated, you don't decide whether to save each month - it happens. When a rule exists that credit is only used for specific categories of spending, you don't negotiate with yourself in the store - the rule has already decided. When investing happens through a recurring contribution, the behavior continues regardless of whether you remembered to initiate it.

The most consistent financial behaviors are almost always the ones that have been made automatic - because automatic behaviors don't require the decision that willpower would otherwise have to protect.

There is a mathematical dimension to consistency that is worth understanding clearly, because it is the most concrete argument for why starting early and continuing steadily produces results that feel disproportionate to the effort involved.

It is called compounding - and while it is most commonly discussed in the context of investing, it applies equally to habits, skills, knowledge, and almost every other domain where small inputs accumulate over time.

Compounding works like this: growth in one period becomes the base on which growth in the next period is calculated. Returns generate returns. Interest earns interest. Small gains produce larger gains, which produce larger gains still - not in a straight line, but in a curve that starts nearly flat and eventually rises steeply.

The reason this curve matters is that most of the growth happens in the later periods - the ones you only reach if you were consistent through the earlier ones when nothing seemed to be happening. People who stop during the flat part of the curve never experience the steep part. They abandoned the process precisely when the process was building the foundation that the later results would stand on.

This is why the person who saves $200 per month from age 22 to age 65 typically ends up with a dramatically larger amount than the person who saves $400 per month from age 35 to age 65 - even though the second person contributed more total dollars. The first person's money had more time in the compounding curve. The flat period, endured consistently, enabled a steep period that the late starter never fully accessed.

Time is the variable that makes consistency powerful.
And the only way to use time effectively is to start before you can see the results - and continue after you've grown tired of not seeing them yet.

Consistency also applies to the habits and patterns that don't involve money directly but shape financial outcomes significantly.
The habit of reviewing your finances regularly - not obsessively, but consistently - means you always have a current, accurate picture of where you stand. Problems are caught early. Drift is noticed before it becomes damage. Decisions are made from clarity rather than assumption.

The habit of learning consistently - reading, listening, asking questions, staying curious about how financial systems work - means your understanding grows steadily alongside your income and your obligations. You are not caught off guard by things you would have known if you had been paying attention.

The habit of making decisions deliberately rather than reactively - pausing before spending, planning before committing, thinking before borrowing - means the pattern of your choices is intentional rather than impulsive. And patterns, made consistently over time, become the architecture of your financial life.

None of these habits are dramatic. None of them require significant time or resources. All of them, applied consistently over years, produce outcomes that feel larger than the individual actions that built them.

There is one more dimension of consistency worth addressing directly - what to do when you break it.

Because you will. Not if - when. There will be months where saving doesn't happen. Weeks where the budget gets ignored. Periods where financial discipline gives way to life's demands, and the consistent behaviors you built get disrupted. This is not failure. It is human. And how you respond to it determines whether a break in consistency becomes a permanent stop or a temporary interruption.

The answer is not to treat every disruption as evidence that you cannot maintain consistency. It is not to wait until January, or until next month, or until a more convenient moment to restart. It is to resume - as quickly as possible, as close to where you left off as possible, without the weight of self-judgment that makes resuming feel harder than it needs to be.

One missed month of saving does not erase a year of consistent contributions. One week of poor spending decisions does not invalidate the patterns you've built. The recovery from a break in consistency is almost always simpler than people make it — it requires only the next right action, taken as soon as possible after the break occurred.

The people who build strong financial lives are not the ones who were perfectly consistent without exception. They are the ones who resumed quickly every time they stopped - who treated consistency as a direction rather than a perfect record, and who never let a temporary break become a permanent one.

If you're between 18 and 22, this is where your patterns are forming. You don't need to do everything perfectly. You need to do something - one thing, consistently - and build from there. The habits you establish now, however modest, will carry forward in ways that become significant simply because of how long they have to compound. One small consistent action, started now, is worth far more than a large ambitious plan that requires perfect conditions to maintain.

If you're between 23 and 30, this is where consistency separates the people who are genuinely building from the people who are earning well but not accumulating anything. Your income is likely real, your obligations are real, and the gap between those who are building and those who are maintaining is increasingly defined by one thing — whether their financial behaviors are consistent or conditional. Make yours consistent. Automate what you can. Build systems that continue when your motivation doesn't. And trust that the flat part of the curve, navigated steadily, leads somewhere worth going.

Think honestly about your current relationship with consistency. Are your financial behaviors conditional - dependent on how you feel, how the month went, how much energy you have - or are they structural, built into the way your money moves regardless of those variables?

If your income increased, would your saving increase automatically, or would it require a new decision in a moment when spending is the easier choice?

If motivation faded - as it will - what systems exist to keep the right behaviors happening anyway?

These are the questions that determine not just what you do when things are going well, but what continues when they aren't.

And what continues when things aren't going well is what actually builds something.

Because progress doesn't come from the moments when everything aligned perfectly and following through felt easy.

It comes from the moments when nothing was particularly inspiring and you did it anyway.

Those moments, accumulated over time, become something remarkable.

Not because any single one of them was -
but because all of them were there.
Every week.
Every month.
Every year.

Quietly building something that eventually becomes impossible to ignore.

That is the power of consistency.
Not dramatic. Not fast. Not exciting in the moment.
But over time - the most powerful force available to you.

What To Do This Week: Identify one financial behavior you want to make consistent - saving a fixed amount, reviewing your budget weekly, making an extra debt payment, contributing to an investment account. Then remove the decision from the moment by automating it or scheduling it as a recurring calendar commitment. The goal is not to rely on remembering or feeling motivated - it is to build a system that continues without requiring either. Start this week. Not next month. This week.

21

DELAYED GRATIFICATION - CHOOSING LATER OVER NOW

There is a pattern that shows up consistently in the financial lives of people who build something meaningful over time - a pattern so simple that it almost doesn't sound like a strategy, and so difficult to maintain that most people abandon it long before it produces its most significant results.

It is the ability to choose later over now.

Not always. Not in every situation. Not in a way that turns life into a joyless exercise in perpetual deferral. But consistently enough, and in the right situations, that the direction of your decisions bends toward building rather than consuming - toward what you are creating rather than only what you are experiencing in this moment.

This is called delayed gratification. And while it sounds straightforward in principle, it runs directly against some of the most powerful forces in modern life - the immediacy of digital purchasing, the constant visibility of what others appear to be enjoying, the very human tendency to weight the present far more heavily than the future when making decisions in real time.

Understanding why it matters - and building the practical habits that make it sustainable - is one of the most valuable things you can do for your financial life at any age.

Aaron was 23 with a steady income and the freedom to direct it however he chose. He spent the way most people his age do - on things that felt good now, experiences that felt worth it in the moment, purchases that seemed reasonable individually and never catastrophic in isolation. There was nothing extreme about his behavior. It was simply present-focused - oriented almost entirely toward what the current moment called for, with little attention to what the accumulation of those moments was building over time.

His friend Daniel earned nearly the same income and lived a comparable lifestyle. But Daniel had developed a habit - small, unglamorous, and entirely invisible from the outside - of pausing before spending. Not every time. Not as a rigid rule that made life feel restrictive. But often enough, and in enough of the right situations, that his decisions tilted slightly but consistently toward the future rather than entirely toward the present.

He waited a few days before buying things he wanted but didn't need. He asked himself, honestly, whether the purchase would still feel worth it a week from now. He saved a portion of every paycheck before spending what remained. He made choices that his present self sometimes resisted but that his future self consistently benefited from.

From the outside, the difference between Aaron and Daniel was invisible for years.

Both were working. Both were living. Both seemed to be doing fine.

But over time, their decisions had been building two different realities.

Aaron's money came and went. When something unexpected happened, he had to scramble - reaching for credit, delaying other obligations, managing the pressure of a financial life with no cushion beneath it. Daniel, without having done anything dramatic or extreme, had built something quiet and significant. His savings had grown. His options had expanded. When the same unexpected situations arose, they were inconveniences rather than crises.

The difference wasn't income.

It wasn't luck.

It was timing - specifically, the consistent willingness to choose what would serve him later over what felt easiest right now.

Delayed gratification is frequently misunderstood as a form of self-denial - the idea that you must sacrifice enjoyment in the present in order to be financially responsible. That framing is both inaccurate and unhelpful, because it sets up an opposition between living well now and building well for later that doesn't actually exist.

The real principle is not denial. It is **intentional timing.**

It is the recognition that not every want needs to be satisfied immediately, that the timing of a purchase or a financial decision matters as much as the decision itself, and that the space between wanting something and acting on that want is where some of the most important financial choices get made - or bypassed entirely.

When you buy something impulsively, you are allowing the feeling of wanting to make the decision. When you pause, you are allowing your judgment to participate. And judgment, given a moment to operate, often produces a different answer than impulse does - not always, but often enough to change the trajectory of your finances over time.

This is not about becoming someone who never spends freely or never enjoys the present. It is about developing enough of a pause between impulse and action that your choices are genuinely yours - made with awareness rather than simply made in the moment the want was felt.

The science behind why delayed gratification is difficult is worth understanding, because knowing why something is hard makes it easier to address without self-judgment.

The human brain is wired to weight immediate rewards more heavily than future ones - a phenomenon psychologists call **temporal discounting.** The further away a reward is in time, the less valuable it feels in the present moment, even if its objective value is significantly higher. This is why a dollar today feels more compelling than two dollars next year, even when the math clearly favors waiting.

This wiring made evolutionary sense in environments where the future was genuinely uncertain and immediate resources were survival-critical. It makes considerably less sense in a modern financial context, where the future is more predictable and where the ability to defer consumption consistently is one of the most reliable paths to long-term financial security.

Understanding this doesn't eliminate the pull of immediate reward. But it contextualizes it - it allows you to recognize the impulse for what it is, a deeply ingrained cognitive tendency rather than an accurate signal of what is actually in your best interest, and to make a deliberate choice rather than simply following the pull automatically.

There are practical habits that make delayed gratification more sustainable - not through willpower alone, but through structure that supports better decisions before the moment of temptation arrives.

The first and most powerful is the **waiting period.** Before making any non-essential purchase above a threshold you define for yourself - it might be $50, it might be $100, it might be $200 - you commit to waiting a fixed period of time before buying. Twenty-four hours for smaller purchases. A week for larger ones. Thirty days for significant ones.

The waiting period does several things simultaneously. It eliminates purely impulsive purchases - the ones that would have happened in the moment and been forgotten or regretted shortly after. It separates the feeling of wanting from the decision to buy, giving your judgment time to participate. And it frequently reveals that what felt urgent in the moment loses its urgency with time - that the want fades naturally without the purchase ever being made. When the want survives the waiting period, the purchase is almost always more satisfying because it was chosen deliberately rather than surrendered to impulsively.

The second habit is **pre-deciding your priorities.** When your financial values are clearly established in advance - when you have decided, before any specific situation arises, what matters most to you and what you are working toward - individual decisions become easier because the framework already exists. You are not negotiating with yourself in the moment. You are simply checking an incoming decision against a set of values you already hold.

This is why the financial clarity exercises throughout this book matter beyond their immediate application. Knowing what you are building, why you are building it, and what you are willing to trade in the short term to get there creates an anchor that holds when the pull of immediate gratification is strong.

The third habit is **making the future concrete.** The reason the future loses to the present in most impulsive financial decisions is that the future is abstract. It is vague, distant, and emotionally flat compared to the vivid, immediate, tangible experience of wanting something now. Making the future more concrete - through specific savings goals attached to specific outcomes, through visual reminders of what you are building toward, through regular reviews of your financial progress that make the trajectory visible - reduces that emotional gap and makes the future feel more real in the moment of decision.

Delayed gratification also operates at a larger scale than individual purchases - and this is where its impact on your financial life becomes most significant.

Every time your income increases and you choose to strengthen your financial foundation before upgrading your lifestyle, you are practicing delayed gratification at scale. Every time you make an extra debt payment instead of using that money for something enjoyable right now, you are trading a present indulgence for a future with less weight. Every time you contribute to a retirement account instead of spending what you could have spent, you are making a choice that your future self will benefit from in ways your present self cannot fully feel.

These larger expressions of the principle are where real financial trajectories are built or not built. The individual purchase decisions matter — they add up, and the habits they reflect are real. But the big-picture willingness to defer lifestyle upgrades, to prioritize building over consuming, and to make decisions based on where you want to be rather than only on what you want right now - that is what separates people who build lasting financial stability from people who earn well but never seem to accumulate anything.

It is also worth addressing the version of delayed gratification that has gone too far - because balance matters here as much as it does anywhere else.

Extreme deferral - refusing every present enjoyment in pursuit of a future that never quite arrives - is not the goal. It is not financially necessary and it is not psychologically sustainable. A financial plan that offers nothing enjoyable in the present will not be maintained, because humans are not built to endure indefinite sacrifice for abstract future benefit. The plan will eventually be abandoned, and with it the progress it was producing.

The goal is not to stop living now in order to live better later.

The goal is to live well now while also building something for later - to find the balance point where the present is genuinely enjoyed and the future is genuinely being built, rather than sacrificing one entirely for the other.

That balance point is different for everyone and shifts as circumstances change. What it requires is not a rigid formula but an honest, ongoing conversation with yourself about whether your current decisions reflect the life you want to be living - both now and eventually.

If you're between 18 and 22, this is where your relationship with delayed gratification is being established. The habits you build around spending, waiting, and deciding now will carry forward into every financial situation you encounter as the stakes get higher. Practicing the pause - even in small, low-stakes situations - builds the muscle that makes it available when the decisions are larger and the temptations are stronger.

If you're between 23 and 30, the impact of your choices in this area is becoming more visible and more significant. This is where the gap between people who wait for the right moment to spend and people who spend at every available moment begins to produce meaningfully different financial realities. The decisions you make consistently in this decade will compound into very different positions by the time you reach your thirties and forties. That is not a distant concern - it is the direct result of what you are doing right now.

Think honestly about your recent pattern of decisions.

When you want something, how much time typically passes between the want and the action? Are your spending decisions made from a place of intention, or from the momentum of the immediate moment? If you traced your last month of discretionary spending, how much of it would you endorse fully on reflection - and how much would you characterize as impulsive, habitual, or driven more by feeling than by genuine choice?

These questions are not meant to generate guilt.

They are meant to generate clarity.

Because clarity, in the moment of a financial decision, is exactly what delayed gratification requires and exactly what impulse bypasses.

The choice between now and later is not made once.

It is made repeatedly - in small moments, large moments, and every moment in between - and the pattern of those choices, accumulated over time, becomes the financial life you are living.

So practice the pause.

Build the habit of waiting before deciding.

Make your priorities clear enough that they can compete with the pull of the present.

And trust that what you are building by choosing later over now is worth more than anything you could have bought by choosing now instead.

Because it is.

Not in a way that feels obvious in the moment.
But in a way that becomes undeniable over time.

And time, as this entire book has argued from the very first page - is always on your side.

If you use it.

What To Do This Week: Identify one category of spending where you consistently act on impulse - food delivery, online shopping, entertainment, clothing, or anything else that comes to mind without much deliberation. For the next seven days, apply a mandatory 24-hour waiting period to every non-essential purchase in that category. Before buying anything, write down what it is, why you want it, and what you will do with the money if you decide not to buy it. At the end of the week, review what you bought, what you didn't, and how you feel about each decision. That review will tell you more about your relationship with delayed gratification than any advice could.

22

DISCIPLINE VS. MOTIVATION

At some point in your financial life - probably more than once - you will feel genuinely inspired to change something. You will read something, hear something, or experience something that creates a surge of clarity and energy around your money. You will see exactly what needs to be done, feel fully committed to doing it, and start with a level of focus that makes the whole project feel not just possible but inevitable.

That feeling is motivation.

And it is real, and valuable, and worth using when it arrives.

The problem is not that motivation exists. The problem is what happens when it leaves - because it always does. Motivation is not a permanent state. It is a weather pattern. It comes and goes based on factors that have nothing to do with how important your financial goals are or how capable you are of reaching them. It responds to results, to energy levels, to stress, to the ordinary friction of daily life. And when it fades - which it will, often at the worst possible moment - whatever you built on it tends to fade with it.

This is why motivation, despite feeling like the engine of change, is actually one of the least reliable foundations for lasting financial behavior.

And why discipline - misunderstood, undervalued, and far less exciting - is the thing that actually builds a life.

Tyler was 25 when he decided, with genuine conviction, that he was going to take control of his finances. He had been thinking about it for a while, and something - a conversation, a number that finally landed differently, a moment of honest reckoning - tipped him into action. He sat down, created a plan, set savings goals, outlined a debt repayment strategy, and committed to making better decisions starting immediately.

The first few weeks were everything he hoped they would be.
He followed the plan. He tracked his spending. He made the right calls consistently and felt the satisfaction of being someone who was finally doing what he knew needed to be done. It felt like a turning point - the kind of before-and-after moment that changes everything.

Then life did what life does.

His schedule got heavier. A stressful period at work consumed the mental energy he had been using for financial awareness. An unexpected expense disrupted the plan. The satisfaction of early progress faded into the quieter, less rewarding experience of simply maintaining behaviors that no longer felt new or energizing.

The motivation that had launched everything began to thin.

And as it thinned, so did the behaviors it had been powering.
Not all at once. Gradually - a skipped budget review here, a missed savings transfer there, a spending decision made without the delibera-

tion he had been applying. The plan was still technically in place. He just wasn't following it the way he had been.

By the time he noticed the drift, he was further from his starting point than felt comfortable to acknowledge. And the familiar cycle began - guilt about the drift, a renewed surge of motivation to correct it, a strong restart, and eventually another fade.

That cycle - motivation, action, fade, restart - is one of the most common and most costly patterns in personal finance. Not because the intentions behind it are wrong, but because motivation was never designed to power something that needs to run indefinitely. Discipline was.

Discipline is not the same thing as willpower, though the two are often conflated. Willpower is an act of active resistance - the conscious effort to override an impulse in a specific moment. It is real and sometimes necessary, but it is also exhausting and finite. Every act of willpower draws on a pool of mental and emotional energy that depletes with use, which is why financial decisions made at the end of a long, stressful day tend to be worse than ones made with a fresh mind.

Discipline, properly understood, is something different. It is not the repeated act of resisting temptation. It is the construction of an environment, a set of systems, and a pattern of behavior in which temptation has less opportunity to operate in the first place.

The disciplined person is not someone who fights their impulses heroically every day. They are someone who has arranged their financial life so that the right behaviors happen by default - automatically, routinely, without requiring a fresh decision and a fresh expenditure of willpower every single time.

This is why the practical applications throughout this book have consistently pointed toward automation, systems, and structure rather than toward trying harder or caring more. Not because effort doesn't matter, but because effort directed toward building a system is worth far more than effort directed toward fighting yourself every day over the same decisions.

When your savings transfer automatically, you don't need discipline to save - the saving happens whether or not you feel like it. When your credit card is paid automatically from a dedicated account, you don't need discipline to pay on time - the payment is already scheduled. When your investment contribution recurs monthly without manual initiation, you don't need discipline to invest - you are already investing.

Discipline, at its most effective, is the work you do once to build a system that runs without you having to be disciplined every day.

That said, systems don't run themselves completely. There are moments in every financial life where a genuine act of discipline - of choosing the harder thing in the moment because it aligns with what you have decided matters - is required. And in those moments, a few principles make the choosing easier.

The first is **clarity of purpose.** Discipline is significantly easier when you know specifically what you are being disciplined toward. A vague commitment to "saving more" or "spending less" provides insufficient anchor when the moment of temptation arrives. A specific commitment - saving $300 per month toward a $5,000 emergency fund that will be in place by December - provides something concrete to weigh against the immediate pull of spending. The more clearly you can see what you are building and why it matters, the more weight the future carries in the present moment of decision.

The second is **removing friction from the right behaviors and adding it to the wrong ones.** Behavioral design - the deliberate structuring of your environment to make good decisions easier and poor ones harder - is one of the most underutilized tools in personal finance. Moving savings out of your checking account immediately after each paycheck removes the friction of the decision to save and adds friction to the decision to spend what's not there. Deleting shopping apps from your phone adds friction to impulsive purchases. Keeping your credit cards out of your digital wallet adds friction to using credit. None of these changes require heroic discipline. They require one good decision that makes subsequent decisions easier.

The third is **tracking progress in a way that makes the direction visible.** One of the reasons discipline fades is that the progress it is producing is invisible - the savings growing slowly in the background, the debt declining incrementally, the financial foundation strengthening in ways that don't announce themselves with immediate reward. Making that progress visible - through a simple tracker, a regular review, a chart that shows where you were and where you are - connects the disciplined behavior to the outcome it is producing and gives the brain the feedback it needs to sustain the behavior without motivation doing all the work.

There is also an important distinction between discipline as a permanent state of self-denial and discipline as a temporary investment in a future with more freedom.

The goal of financial discipline is not to live under restriction forever. It is to build, through a period of intentional behavior, a financial foundation strong enough that future decisions carry less weight and create less stress. The person who lives disciplined financial habits in their twenties and thirties is typically the person who has genuine financial freedom in their forties and fifties - not because they deprived themselves, but because they invested in a future where choices are made from abundance rather than from constraint.

Discipline, in this framing, is not the opposite of freedom. It is the path to it.

The person who spends freely in their twenties because restriction feels unacceptable often finds, in their forties, that they are more restricted than ever - by debt, by insufficient savings, by a financial structure that requires them to keep working at the same pace indefinitely because nothing was built to support an alternative.

The relationship between present discipline and future freedom is direct, even if it is not always visible in the moments when discipline is being exercised.

There is one more dimension of the discipline conversation that deserves honest acknowledgment: the role of identity.

The most durable form of discipline is not the kind that comes from trying to do the right thing. It is the kind that comes from being someone who does the right thing - from having internalized the financial behaviors you want to maintain as part of who you are rather than as external rules you are trying to comply with.

When saving is something you do because you are a person who saves, rather than something you are forcing yourself to do despite wanting to spend, the behavior becomes significantly more sustainable. The identity supports the action rather than fighting it. And identity, unlike motivation, is relatively stable - it doesn't depend on how you feel on a given day or how much energy you have available.

Building financial identity is not a mystical process. It happens through the same mechanism everything in this book has described: small, consistent actions, repeated over time, that become the evidence you collect about who you are.

Every time you follow through on a saving commitment, you are telling yourself a story about the kind of person you are. Every time you make a deliberate financial decision rather than an impulsive one, you are reinforcing an identity. Every time you honor a financial value under pressure, you are building the self-concept that makes honoring it next time slightly easier.

This is why the early actions matter beyond their direct financial impact. They are not just building savings or reducing debt. They are building the financial identity that will make every subsequent action more natural, more sustainable, and less dependent on motivation showing up when you need it.

If you're between 18 and 22, this is the period when your financial identity and your financial habits are being established simultaneously. The behaviors you practice now are not just producing small financial results - they are forming the person who will make financial decisions for the next several decades. The discipline you build now is not temporary scaffolding. It is the foundation of who you become. Take it seriously, not as a burden, but as an investment in a version of yourself that will thank you in ways you cannot yet fully imagine.

If you're between 23 and 30, the gap between disciplined financial behavior and motivation-dependent financial behavior is beginning to produce visible results in the lives of the people around you. This is the decade where the patterns become entrenched - where the person who built systems and habits in their early twenties begins to experience the compounding benefits of having done so, and where the person who relied on motivation begins to feel the compounding cost of having not. It is not too late to build the discipline that changes your trajectory. But the sooner you build it, the more of the compounding benefit you capture.

Take an honest look at your current financial behaviors and ask yourself which ones are system-dependent and which ones are motivation-dependent.

The system-dependent ones - the behaviors that happen automatically, regardless of how you feel - are your most reliable assets. They are the behaviors that will still be running when motivation is nowhere to be found.

The motivation-dependent ones - the behaviors that happen when you feel inspired and stop when you don't - are your vulnerabilities. They are the gaps where financial progress stalls during the inevitable periods when life is hard and motivation is scarce.

The work of discipline is to convert as many of the second category into the first as possible.

Not through heroic effort.
Through systems.
Through structure.

Through the one-time decision that makes the ongoing decision unnecessary.

Because motivation will come and go for the rest of your life.
And on the days it goes - the systems you built are what keep you moving.

The structure you created is what holds the direction.

The discipline you developed is what separates the life you are building from the life that simply happened to you.

So build the systems.
Create the structure.
Develop the discipline.
And then - let it run.

Because the goal was never to be motivated every day.

The goal was to build something that keeps building - even on the days when you aren't.

What To Do This Week: Identify one financial behavior that currently depends entirely on motivation - something you do when you feel like it and skip when you don't. Then spend fifteen minutes this week converting it into a system. Automate it, schedule it as a recurring calendar commitment, or create a structural change that makes the right behavior the default rather than the deliberate choice. One behavior, made automatic. That is this week's work. And it is more valuable than any amount of renewed motivation.

PART VI

THE LONG GAME

23

THE COST OF WAITING

Every decision you make has a cost. That much is obvious. What is less obvious - and what catches most people off guard - is that every decision you delay has a cost too. A cost that is real, that accumulates, and that is almost never visible in the moment the delay is chosen.

This is what makes waiting so seductive as a strategy. It doesn't feel like a strategy at all. It feels like a neutral holding position - a pause that costs nothing because nothing bad is actively happening. You are not spending recklessly. You are not making obvious mistakes. You are simply not yet doing the things you know you should be doing. And because the consequences of that inaction don't announce themselves immediately, the delay feels harmless.

It isn't.

Every month you delay starting an emergency fund is a month you remain exposed to the financial damage an unexpected event can cause. Every month you delay contributing to a retirement account is a month of compounding that belongs to someone else's future, not

yours. Every month you carry a high-interest balance without an aggressive repayment strategy is a month of interest charges that reduce your ability to build anything else. Every month you delay learning how credit works is a month your financial reputation is being shaped without your awareness or intention.
None of these costs are dramatic in isolation. Together, over time, they are enormous.

Ryan was 26 and aware - genuinely, honestly aware - that there were things he needed to address. His finances were not in crisis, but they were not where he wanted them to be either. He knew he should be saving more consistently. He knew his credit needed attention. He knew that the retirement contributions he kept meaning to start hadn't started. He knew that the financial habits he had been meaning to build were still unmade.

He also knew, or told himself he knew, that he would get to all of it. When things slowed down. When work felt less demanding. When the month felt less tight. When he felt more ready.

Those conditions never quite arrived - not because his life was uniquely difficult, but because life is not structured to deliver the convenient pause that waiting depends on. The busy months were followed by other busy months. The tight months were followed by months with different but equally real competing demands. The readiness he was waiting to feel was always just slightly out of reach, perpetually deferred by the friction of the present moment.

Years passed.

And when he finally sat down and looked honestly at where he was versus where he would have been if he had started when he first knew he should, the gap was sobering.

Not catastrophic. But real. And now more expensive to close than it would have been to prevent.

That is the cost of waiting - not a cliff edge you fall off suddenly, but a gap that widens gradually, quietly, and without drama, until the distance between where you are and where you could have been becomes impossible to dismiss.

The psychology of waiting is worth understanding clearly, because the tendency to delay is not a character flaw or a failure of intelligence. It is a predictable response to a specific set of cognitive patterns that affect almost everyone.

The first is **present bias** - the same temporal discounting discussed in the previous chapter, applied not just to spending but to action. Starting something today requires real effort in the present. The benefit of having started accrues in the future.

Because the present is immediate and the future is abstract, the effort feels disproportionately large relative to the reward, even when the math strongly favors acting now.

The second is **optimism bias** - the consistent human tendency to believe that future circumstances will be more favorable than present ones. Future-me will have more time. Future-me will have more money. Future-me will have more energy and less stress and a clearer picture of what to do. This belief is almost never accurate - not because things don't improve, but because future circumstances bring their own demands and complications that present-me cannot fully anticipate. The conditions that feel like prerequisites for starting are rarely as present in the future as they seem like they should be.

The third is **status quo bias** - the preference for the current state of affairs simply because it is familiar. Changing financial behavior requires disrupting a pattern that, however suboptimal, is at least known. The unknown of a new pattern feels riskier than the known cost of the current one, even when the current pattern is actively working against you.

Understanding these patterns doesn't eliminate them. But naming them creates a small but meaningful distance between the impulse to wait and the decision of whether to act on it. That distance is where your judgment has the opportunity to override what your instincts are recommending.

There is a specific dimension of waiting that deserves particular attention in the context of this book: the cost of waiting to learn.
Most of the financial mistakes people make are not the result of bad intentions or reckless behavior. They are the result of operating in systems they don't understand - making decisions about credit, debt, taxes, insurance, and investing without the foundational knowledge that would have changed those decisions, because no one taught them and they hadn't yet sought it out.

The longer you wait to develop financial literacy, the more decisions you make from that place of incomplete understanding. And decisions made without understanding don't wait for understanding to catch up - they produce consequences that compound just as effectively as good decisions do, simply in the wrong direction.

This is why learning - reading, asking questions, paying attention to how financial systems work - is not a passive background activity. It is one of the most financially valuable things you can do at any stage of your life, and the earlier you do it, the longer you have to apply what you learn before the stakes get high and the margin for error gets small.

Every chapter of this book is an argument for the same thing: start before you need to. Learn before it's required. Build before the pressure arrives. Not because difficulty is coming - though it is - but because building before it arrives is always cheaper, easier, and more effective than building in response to it.

~

The antidote to waiting is not urgency - it is not replacing a passive holding pattern with anxious, reactive action. It is something quieter and more sustainable.

It is starting.

Starting with whatever is available. Starting with whatever is understood. Starting imperfectly, incompletely, without a full plan and without the certainty that everything is being done correctly. Starting because the alternative - continuing to wait for conditions that will not arrive on their own - is more expensive than the imperfection of beginning.

A practical approach to overcoming the inertia of waiting is to make the first action as small as possible. Not the first action of a complete financial overhaul. The first action of one thing. Open the savings account. Pull the credit report. Log in to StudentAid.gov. Transfer $50 into a dedicated account. Spend fifteen minutes reading about Roth IRAs.

Small first actions have a property that large first actions do not: they are actually taken. And action - any action in the right direction - breaks the psychological grip of waiting in a way that planning and intending and meaning to never do. Once you have done one thing, the next thing is easier. Momentum is real, and it begins with a single step rather than a perfect plan.

There is also a reframe worth carrying into every future moment when waiting feels like a reasonable choice.

Waiting is not neutral. It is a decision.

Every day you choose not to start saving is a day you chose not to save. Every month you choose not to address your credit is a month you chose to let it develop without your participation. Every year you choose not to begin building for retirement is a year you chose to reduce the amount of time that money has to grow.

These are choices. They have outcomes. And the outcomes accumulate in exactly the same way that the outcomes of good decisions do - just in the opposite direction.

When waiting is understood as a decision rather than an absence of one, it becomes subject to the same evaluation as any other decision: is this the choice I want to make, knowing what it costs? Sometimes the answer is genuinely yes - not all delays are harmful, and prioritization is a real and necessary skill. But often, when the cost of waiting is made explicit and specific rather than vague and abstract, the answer changes.

And when the answer changes, the behavior changes with it.

If you're between 18 and 22, the cost of waiting is currently at its lowest point it will ever be - because time is at its most abundant. Every financial behavior you begin now has the maximum possible runway to compound, to develop, to produce results that would be significantly harder to replicate if you start later. The actions available to you right now are not smaller than they will be later. They are more powerful, because they have more time. Use that. Not perfectly - just consistently, and starting now.

If you're between 23 and 30, you may already feel some of the cost of having waited on certain things. That feeling is useful information — not as a source of regret, but as a concrete illustration of why starting now matters more than starting perfectly. The gap is still closeable. The trajectory is still shapeable. But the window in which closing the gap is easy is narrowing, and every month of additional delay makes the work of catching up incrementally more significant. Start now. Close the gap. And then build far enough ahead that waiting is never again the choice you're making by default.

Look honestly at the things you have been waiting to address.
Not in general. Specifically.

The savings you have been meaning to start. The credit report you have been meaning to pull. The retirement account you have been meaning to open. The debt repayment plan you have been meaning to create. The insurance you have been meaning to evaluate. The financial conversation you have been meaning to have.

Pick one.

Not the easiest one. Not the most comfortable one. The one whose delay is costing you the most - in money, in exposure, in the compounding gap between where you are and where you would be if you had started six months ago.

Then do one thing toward it today.

Not a plan to do something. Not a commitment to start soon. One action, taken today, that moves the thing forward from the category of waiting into the category of begun.

Because begun, even imperfectly, is worth more than intended, no matter how seriously the intention was held.

The best time to start was earlier.
You cannot have that time back.
But the next best time is a fact that is always true -
and always now.

What To Do This Week: Make a list of every financial thing you have been meaning to address but haven't. Write them all down - savings, credit, retirement, debt, insurance, taxes, anything that belongs on the list. Then rank them by cost of continued delay - which one is actively getting more expensive or more damaging the longer it goes unaddressed? That one goes first. Identify the single smallest action that would move it forward, and take that action before the week is over. Not a plan. An action. The list will still be there. But one item on it will no longer be waiting.

24

WHERE MOST PEOPLE END UP - AND WHY

If you pay close attention to the people around you over a long enough period of time, something becomes visible that isn't obvious in the short term. You begin to see that where people end up financially is rarely random. It is rarely the result of catastrophic bad luck or extraordinary good fortune. It is, in most cases, the direct and predictable result of patterns - patterns of behavior, patterns of thinking, patterns of decision-making that were running quietly in the background for years before their destination became clear.

This is both the most sobering and the most empowering insight in personal finance.

Sobering because it means that the financial difficulties most people experience in their thirties, forties, and beyond were largely built - incrementally, invisibly, through decisions that seemed reasonable at the time - in the years before those difficulties arrived. Not through dramatic failure. Through the slow accumulation of patterns that were never examined closely enough to be corrected.

Empowering because it means the same thing in reverse: the financial stability, freedom, and security that some people build is also not accidental. It is also the result of patterns - different ones, applied consistently over the same period of time. And patterns, unlike luck, are within your control.

Anthony was 35 when he looked honestly at his financial life and couldn't find a single catastrophic mistake to blame for where he was.

That was the most disorienting part.

He hadn't made obviously reckless decisions. He hadn't gambled his savings away or trusted the wrong person with his money or experienced some dramatic reversal that explained the gap between where he was and where he had imagined he would be by this point. He had simply lived the way most people live - earning, spending, occasionally saving when it felt convenient, borrowing when it felt necessary, and assuming, throughout most of it, that things would gradually come together in a way that justified the lack of deliberate structure.

They hadn't.

His income had grown over the years, but his expenses had grown with it. His lifestyle was comfortable but not stable - built on the requirement that the income kept coming at the same level, with very little beneath it if something changed. His retirement contributions were minimal because there had always been something more immediate competing for the money. His credit was functional but not strong. His savings were present but not meaningful.

Nothing was broken. But nothing was built, either.

When he looked at the people he knew who were in genuinely different positions — more stable, more flexible, more in control of what happened to them when life shifted - he couldn't find a dramatic difference in their circumstances that explained it. Similar incomes. Similar educations. Similar starting points.

What was different was their patterns.

The way they had thought about money in their twenties. The habits they had built and maintained. The decisions they had made consistently, not dramatically but repeatedly, in the direction of building something rather than simply maintaining whatever the present moment required.

That gap - between where consistent intentional patterns lead and where unexamined default patterns lead - is where most of the difference in financial outcomes lives. Not in luck. Not in privilege, though privilege is real and matters. In patterns, repeated over time, producing outcomes that were always their natural destination.

The patterns that lead most people to financial difficulty in their later years are not exotic or unusual. They are the default patterns of a culture that teaches people how to earn but rarely teaches them how to manage what they earn. They are the patterns of intelligent, capable people who were simply never given a clear picture of where those patterns were leading.

Earning and spending without structure is the most common. Income arrives, expenses absorb it, and the cycle resets. There is no intentional direction - no predetermined portion that saves, no system that builds. Money flows in and flows out, and whatever remains at the end of the month, if anything, is available for everything else it was never directed toward. Over years, this pattern produces an income that sustains a lifestyle but builds nothing beneath it - no cushion, no foundation, no growing asset base that would make the future less dependent on the income continuing unchanged.

Delaying important decisions indefinitely is the second. The savings account that will be opened next month. The retirement contributions that will start when the income increases. The credit situation that will be addressed when things settle down. The financial education that will happen when there's more time. Each delay feels temporary in the moment. Collectively, they represent years of foregone progress that cannot be recovered by simply starting later with more urgency.

Reacting rather than preparing is the third. Financial life managed entirely in response to what has already happened - expenses that weren't anticipated, situations that weren't prepared for, emergencies that land without a cushion to absorb them. Every reaction has a cost. Credit used to bridge gaps accumulates interest. Problems that grow unaddressed become more expensive to solve. Time spent managing consequences is time not spent building what would have prevented them.

Allowing lifestyle to consume every income increase is the fourth - the pattern described in detail in the lifestyle creep chapter. Income grows, expenses grow to match it, and the financial position remains essentially unchanged at a higher cost level. The raise that could have accelerated debt repayment becomes a better apartment. The promotion that could have funded retirement becomes a newer car. Progress in income produces no progress in financial foundation because every gain is immediately converted into a higher baseline of spending.

Treating money as something to manage rather than something to direct is the fifth and perhaps most fundamental. The difference between managing money and directing it is the difference between responding to where it goes and deciding in advance where it will go. Managing is reactive. Directing is intentional. And the financial life that results from decades of managing is categorically different from the one that results from decades of directing - even when the income is identical.

None of these patterns require bad intentions to run. They run on autopilot, in the absence of deliberate design, because they are the path of least resistance in a world that constantly encourages spending, rarely encourages saving, and almost never teaches people how the systems around them actually work until those systems have already produced consequences that are difficult to reverse.

This is not an excuse. It is context.

Because context matters when it comes to patterns - understanding why a pattern exists is the first step toward being able to change it. The person who recognizes their financial default patterns for what they are - not personal failures, but predictable responses to a lack of early financial education and intentional design - is in a far better position to change those patterns than the person who carries them as evidence of inadequacy.

The patterns are not permanent. They are changeable. And they change through the same mechanism that built them in the first place: repetition, over time, in a consistent direction.

At the same time, it is worth being honest about the version of this story that goes differently.

Because it does go differently - not for everyone, not without effort, but for the people who build and maintain the patterns that lead somewhere better.

Those patterns are also not exotic.

Saving consistently before spending rather than saving what's left over. This single reversal - treating saving as the first obligation rather than the last - is the structural foundation of almost every strong financial position. It doesn't require a large income. It requires a decision, made once and maintained, that some portion of every dollar earned is directed toward the future before the present has a chance to consume it.

Building and managing credit deliberately rather than ignoring it until it becomes a problem. The people with strong credit profiles in their thirties and forties are almost universally the people who began paying attention in their twenties - not because they were financially sophisticated, but because they understood early that their credit history was being built whether they participated in the building or not, and they chose to participate.

Preparing for the unexpected rather than reacting to it - through emergency funds, through insurance, through the general orientation of building before the pressure arrives rather than scrambling after it does. This preparation doesn't prevent difficult moments. It prevents difficult moments from becoming financial disasters.

Keeping lifestyle growth slower than income growth - allowing some increase in standard of living as income rises while directing a meaningful portion of every income increase toward savings, investments, and debt reduction rather than toward lifestyle expansion. The people who build genuine financial security are not the ones who denied themselves everything while their income grew. They are the ones who grew their financial foundation alongside their lifestyle, rather than letting lifestyle consume every gain.

Making financial decisions from a place of understanding rather than assumption - knowing how credit works, how taxes work, how investment compounding works, how insurance protects, how debt accumulates. Understanding the systems that govern financial life means operating within them intentionally rather than being shaped by them unconsciously.

These patterns, maintained consistently over the years when they feel unremarkable and produce invisible results, are what eventually become the financial position that looks, from the outside, like security, stability, and control.

The uncomfortable truth at the center of this chapter is simple: where most people end up is not a mystery. It is the destination their patterns were always pointing toward - a destination that was visible, if anyone had looked closely enough at the direction, years before it arrived.

And the equally important truth is this: you are not most people yet.

You are in the period when the patterns are still forming. When the habits are still being built. When the direction is still genuinely shapeable — not in theory, not in some abstract sense, but practically and specifically, through the decisions you make this month and next month and the month after that.

The people who end up in genuinely different positions than the average are not people with extraordinary advantages. They are people who, at some point early enough to matter, looked honestly at where their patterns were pointing - and made the deliberate choice to point them somewhere better.

That choice is available to you.

It does not require perfection.
It does not require a dramatic overhaul of everything at once.
It requires only the willingness to see your current patterns clearly, to evaluate honestly where they are leading, and to begin making small, consistent adjustments in the direction of where you actually want to go.

If you're between 18 and 22, you are in the most powerful position possible. Your patterns are still being formed. Nothing is yet entrenched. The habits you build now will compound over decades in exactly the same way that financial returns compound - producing results that will feel disproportionate to the effort they required, simply because they were built early enough to have time to grow. You do not have to wait until you are 35 and looking back at what wasn't built to understand the value of starting now.

You are reading this now. Act on it now.

If you're between 23 and 30, your patterns are becoming more defined - but they are not yet fixed. This is the decade where course corrections are still relatively inexpensive and relatively straightforward. The financial habits you establish and maintain in this window will determine, more than almost any other factor, what your financial life looks like at 40, at 50, and beyond. The work required now is real. But it is a fraction of the work that will be required later if nothing changes.

Think honestly about the patterns you are currently running.

Not the intentions. The patterns.

What does your money actually do when it arrives - where does it go, in what order, toward what purposes? Are you saving before spending, or spending before saving - or not saving at all? Are you building credit deliberately, or letting it develop without your participation? Are you preparing for the unexpected, or hoping it doesn't arrive before you're ready? Is your lifestyle growing with your income, or is your financial foundation growing alongside it?

These questions have honest answers.

And honest answers, examined clearly, are the beginning of being able to change what isn't working before it compounds into something larger.

Because where you end up is not yet determined.

It is being determined - right now, through the patterns you are running, the habits you are building, and the decisions you are making in the ordinary, unremarkable moments that don't feel like they matter individually but that collectively become the architecture of your financial life.

That architecture is being built whether you are designing it or not.
The only question is whether you are the architect -
or whether you are simply living in whatever gets built without you.

Choose to be the architect.
The blueprints are in your hands.
And the building has already begun.

What To Do This Week: Set aside thirty minutes this week to do an honest pattern audit. Write down your answers to these five questions: Where does my money go within the first week of receiving it? What percentage of my income do I consistently save? How would I describe my relationship with credit - deliberate or reactive? If my income stopped tomorrow, how many months could I sustain my current life? And if nothing about my current financial behavior changed, where would I realistically be in ten years? Don't filter the answers toward what you wish were true. Write what is actually true. That honesty is the starting point for everything that changes from here.

25

THE LIFE YOU CAN BUILD IF YOU START NOW

Every chapter in this book has shown you what happens when preparation is absent - the pressure that builds, the options that narrow, the compounding cost of patterns that were never examined or corrected. That picture is real and worth understanding clearly. But it is only half of the picture.

The other half - the more important half - is what becomes possible when you do start. When the habits are built early, when the decisions are made intentionally, when the small consistent actions are taken before the pressure arrives to force them. Because the same compounding that works against people who delay works powerfully for the people who begin.

This chapter is about that version of the story.

Not as motivation. Not as a promise that everything will be easy or that the right financial habits will eliminate difficulty from your life. But as a clear, honest picture of what is genuinely available to you - the specific, tangible outcomes that become accessible when the principles in this book are applied consistently, starting now, from wherever you currently are.

Marcus was 30 when he realized something that didn't announce itself dramatically but settled over him with the quiet weight of something true.

He wasn't wealthy. He hadn't made any extraordinary moves. He hadn't received an inheritance or landed a windfall or benefited from timing the market at exactly the right moment. His income was solid but not exceptional. His life, from the outside, looked fairly ordinary.

But something about it felt fundamentally different from the lives of many people around him.

It felt stable.

When something unexpected came up - a car repair, a medical expense, a period of reduced income - he handled it. Not without any stress, but without the kind of cascading financial damage that turns a single bad month into a year of recovery. When an opportunity appeared - a chance to take a risk professionally, a chance to invest in something promising, a chance to make a decision that required resources rather than debt - he could consider it. Not always act on it, but genuinely consider it from a place of choice rather than a place of impossibility.

When he looked at his monthly finances, money was going somewhere meaningful. His retirement account was growing steadily. His emergency fund was solid. His debt was manageable and declining. His credit was strong. And none of it had required a dramatic intervention or a life-changing windfall. It had been built gradually, quietly, through habits established years earlier when the amounts were small and the results were invisible.

That gradual, quiet building - that is the life available to you. Not a life without challenges. A life with a foundation beneath you when challenges arrive. Not a life without constraints. A life where constraints are chosen rather than imposed. Not a life of extraordinary wealth, necessarily - though the habits that build stability are the same habits that build wealth over longer timescales. A life of genuine control over the decisions that shape your daily reality.

That is what starting now actually produces.

Not immediately. Over time. But time, as this entire book has argued, is exactly what you have.

Let's be specific about what starting now - today, this week, this month — actually makes possible over the years ahead. Because the abstract promise of a better future is less useful than a concrete picture of what better actually looks like.

A funded emergency fund means that when your car breaks down, when your health requires unexpected attention, when your income shifts without warning, the situation is a problem rather than a crisis. It is handled from a position of preparation rather than scrambled for in a state of panic. The quality of life difference between those two experiences - between absorbing a shock and being destabilized by it - is not small. It is the difference between a difficult week and a difficult year.

A strong credit profile means that when you are ready to rent a better apartment, finance a vehicle, purchase a home, or access capital for an opportunity that requires it, the doors open rather than close. The interest rates available to you are lower, which means the same borrowed dollar costs you significantly less over time. The options available to you are broader. The negotiating position you occupy is stronger. None of that happens by accident.

It happens because someone paid attention to credit before they needed those doors to be open - and kept paying attention consistently enough that by the time they arrived at the door, the key was already in hand.

Growing retirement contributions - even modest ones, started early - mean that the compounding curve described throughout this book has had time to do its most powerful work. The person who contributes consistently from their mid-twenties does not need to contribute dramatically more per month than the person who starts in their mid-thirties to end up with dramatically more by retirement. The early contributions had more time in the compounding curve. The math is not complicated. But it is unforgiving - in both directions. It rewards early starters disproportionately and penalizes late starters similarly. Starting now, with whatever amount is currently possible, is always better than starting later with more.

Manageable and declining debt means that the portion of your monthly income committed to the past - to paying for decisions already made - is shrinking rather than growing. As it shrinks, the portion available for the present and the future expands. That expansion is not a luxury. It is the financial breathing room that makes everything else more possible - more saving, more investing, more flexibility, more ability to respond to opportunity rather than being locked into obligation.

Intentional spending habits - the discipline of directing money rather than simply watching it leave - mean that your lifestyle is genuinely affordable rather than technically financed. It means that what you own and how you live is funded by your income rather than supported by debt. It means that the choices you make about how to live are actually choices rather than defaults driven by the momentum of spending patterns that were never examined.

Financial literacy - the understanding of how credit, taxes, insurance, investing, and debt actually work - means that you are navigating the financial systems around you with awareness rather than being shaped by them unconsciously. Every piece of understanding you develop is a tool that reduces the cost of future decisions. The person who understands how compound interest works on debt pays less of it. The person who understands tax-advantaged retirement accounts uses them. The person who understands how insurance works is protected by it rather than blindsided by its absence.

These outcomes are not reserved for people with exceptional incomes or exceptional circumstances. They are the natural results of habits applied consistently over time - habits that are available to almost anyone willing to begin and willing to continue.

There is a version of your financial future that most people don't fully allow themselves to imagine - not because it is unrealistic, but because it requires believing that the small actions available to you right now are powerful enough to build something significant over time. That belief is difficult to sustain in the early stages, when the actions feel small and the results are invisible and the gap between where you are and where you want to be feels large.

But the belief is accurate.

The small actions are powerful enough.

Not because of what they produce immediately, but because of what they produce when they are maintained long enough to compound. The $50 per month invested at 22 is not $50 per month invested at 22. It is the $50 per month, and the returns on that $50, and the returns on those returns, across four decades of compounding - a number that bears almost no resemblance to the original contribution.

The one on-time credit card payment is not one payment. It is one payment that becomes part of a pattern that becomes a credit history that becomes a score that becomes access to opportunities at favorable terms for decades.

The emergency fund that starts at $200 and grows by $50 per month is not a slow, insignificant savings effort. It is the foundation of a financial cushion that will absorb shocks that would otherwise require years of credit card debt to recover from.

None of these things are visible in the moment they begin. They become visible over time - and when they do, they look much larger than the actions that created them, because compounding multiplies small consistent inputs into significant outputs in ways that are difficult to intuit until you have experienced them.

You have to trust the process through the period when the results aren't yet visible.

That trust is built by understanding what is happening even when you can't see it - by knowing that the foundation is being laid, that the compounding curve is running, that the habits are doing their work even when the bank balance doesn't yet reflect it dramatically.

And then, at some point, the curve begins to steepen.

The results become visible.

The foundation becomes something you can stand on clearly.
And the distance between where you are and where you would have been without those habits becomes undeniable.

It is also worth being honest about what starting now does not promise.

It does not promise a life without financial difficulty. Unexpected events will happen. Income will fluctuate. Expenses will arise that weren't planned for. Markets will decline. Circumstances will change in ways that even careful preparation cannot fully anticipate.

What starting now promises is not the absence of difficulty. It is a better position from which to face it. A cushion between you and the full force of what life delivers. More options when options matter most. More time to recover when recovery is needed. More control over the decisions that shape your experience - not complete control, but meaningfully more than the person who waited has.

That difference - between facing difficulty prepared and facing it exposed - is not a small one. It is the difference that determines whether a hard period becomes a temporary setback or a lasting derailment. And it is built, or not built, in the years before the difficulty arrives.

The life you can build if you start now is not a fantasy. It is not a promise of perfection or the guarantee of an outcome that eliminates all financial stress from your existence. It is something more valuable than either of those things.

It is a trajectory.

A direction that, maintained consistently over time, leads to a financial life characterized by stability rather than fragility, by choice rather than constraint, by preparation rather than perpetual reaction. A life where money is a tool you direct rather than a force that directs you. A life where the unexpected is inconvenient rather than devastating. A life where the future is something you are building toward rather than something you are hoping will somehow be better than the present.

That life is built from decisions that are available to you right now. Not special decisions. Not large ones. The ordinary, unglamorous decisions that appear throughout every chapter of this book - to save before spending, to manage credit deliberately, to build an emergency fund, to understand taxes, to protect what you're building with insurance, to choose your environment with intention, to practice delayed gratification, to build discipline rather than depend on motivation.

These decisions, made consistently, over time, from wherever you currently are - that is the life.

If you're between 18 and 22, you are standing at the beginning of the most powerful financial window of your life. The habits you build right now will have more time to compound than any habit you build later. The foundation you lay right now will support more than any foundation built under pressure. The patterns you establish right now will carry forward into every subsequent decade of your financial life, shaping outcomes in ways that will feel, eventually, far larger than the actions that created them. You do not need to have everything figured out. You need to begin, and you need to continue. That is enough to build something significant.

If you're between 23 and 30, the window is still wide open - but it is a window, and it does not stay open indefinitely. The financial habits established in this decade have a compounding runway that the habits of the next decade will not. The course corrections made now are less expensive than the ones that will need to be made later. The foundation built now will support the increasingly significant financial decisions that the coming decade will bring. This is the time to take what you understand and apply it - not perfectly, not all at once, but consistently and with genuine intention.

Take a moment to think about the financial life you actually want. Not in vague terms. Specifically.

What does financial stability feel like in your daily life? What does it mean to handle an unexpected expense without it becoming a crisis? What does it feel like to look at your retirement account and see something growing? What does it feel like to have options - to be able to consider an opportunity, make a choice, take a calculated risk - from a position of preparation rather than desperation?

That feeling. That specific, concrete experience of a financial life that is working rather than constantly requiring management just to stay in place.

That is what you are building toward.

And it is built from what you do today.

Not from what you intend. Not from what you plan to do eventually. From what you actually do, consistently, starting now.

So start.

Not when you feel ready.
Not when the amount feels significant.
Not when the plan feels complete.
Start with what you have, where you are, with the understanding you currently possess.

And then keep going.

Because the life you can build if you start now is not a distant destination.

It is a direction.

And every step you take in that direction - however small, however imperfect, however unremarkable in the moment it is taken -

is building something.
Something that compounds.
Something that grows.

Something that eventually becomes the financial life you chose to create rather than the one that simply happened to you.

That is the life available to you.

It starts now.

What To Do This Week: Write down, specifically, what financial stability looks like for you in five years. Not a vague aspiration - a concrete picture. What is your emergency fund balance? What is your retirement account balance? What does your credit score look like? What debt, if any, do you still carry? What does your monthly financial structure look like - what goes where, in what order, toward what purposes? Then identify the single most important habit you need to build right now to move toward that picture. Not ten habits. One. The most important one. Begin it this week. And let everything else build from there.

26

THE CHECKLIST - WHAT TO DO WHILE YOU'RE STILL YOUNG

Every chapter in this book has been building toward this one.
Not because a checklist is the most sophisticated financial tool available to you - it isn't. But because sophistication without application produces nothing. Because understanding without action changes nothing. Because the most common reason people who genuinely want to build a better financial life fail to do so is not a lack of information or a lack of intelligence or a lack of desire.

It is the gap between knowing and doing.

This chapter exists to close that gap.

Lauren was 27 when she came to an honest and uncomfortable realization about herself.

She knew things. Real things - not surface-level platitudes, but genuine, substantive understanding of how credit worked, why saving mattered, what debt cost over time, how insurance protected what she was building. She had read, listened, absorbed, and internalized more financial knowledge than most people she knew.

And yet, almost none of it had changed her actual behavior.

Her savings were inconsistent. Her credit was functional but not strong. Her emergency fund existed in theory more than in practice. Her retirement contributions, which she had been intending to start for two years, still hadn't started. The knowledge was real. The application of it was nearly nonexistent.

When she sat with that honestly - really sat with it, without the comfortable buffer of telling herself she just needed to learn a little more before she was ready to act - she recognized the pattern for what it was.

She wasn't waiting for understanding. She had understanding. She was waiting for something else - some external signal, some feeling of readiness, some moment when beginning would feel less like a decision and more like an obvious inevitability.

That moment wasn't coming.

So she stopped waiting for it.

She picked one area. Just one - not the most important one, not the one that would make the biggest difference, just the one that felt most immediately addressable. She opened the savings account she had been meaning to open. She set up the automatic transfer she had been meaning to set up. She did one thing, completely, and let that be enough for that week.

Then she did another thing the following week.

And another after that.

Not a transformation. Not an overhaul. A sequence of single steps, each one modest, each one completed, each one creating a small increment of momentum that made the next step slightly easier than the last.

Within a few months, the financial life she had been intending to build for years had begun to actually exist.

Not because she finally learned something she didn't already know.

Because she finally did something with what she already knew.
That is what this chapter is for.

What follows is a structured checklist - organized by area, applicable regardless of where you currently are, and designed to give you the clearest possible picture of what actually needs to be done. Not everything on this list needs to happen this week. Not everything needs to happen this month. But everything on this list needs to happen - and the sooner each item moves from pending to complete, the stronger your financial foundation becomes.

Work through it honestly. Mark what you have genuinely addressed. Be specific about what remains. And then - most importantly - begin.

AREA 1: FOUNDATIONAL AWARENESS

The starting point of every good financial decision is a clear, accurate picture of your current situation. Without it, every other step is built on assumption rather than reality.

Know your income. Not approximately - specifically. What arrives in your account each month, from every source, after taxes. If your income is variable, calculate a realistic average based on the last three to six months.

Know your expenses. Every one of them. Fixed expenses - rent, insurance, loan payments, subscriptions - and variable ones - food, transportation, entertainment, personal spending. If you have not tracked your spending for at least one full month, do it before moving to anything else. You cannot direct money you haven't accounted for.

Know your net worth. This is simply the total of what you own minus the total of what you owe. List every asset - savings accounts, investment accounts, retirement accounts, the value of any property you own. List every liability - credit card balances, student loans, car loans, any other debt. Subtract the second from the first. The number, whether positive or negative, is your current financial position. It is your starting point. And a starting point, however uncomfortable, is always better than a guess.

Review this picture regularly. Monthly at minimum. Not obsessively - but consistently. Your financial situation is not static, and decisions made with outdated information are decisions made in the dark.

AREA 2: SAVING

Saving is the behavior that everything else in your financial life is built on. Without it, every unexpected expense becomes a crisis, every opportunity requires borrowing, and the future remains entirely dependent on whatever the present happens to deliver.

Save before you spend. Not with what's left over - first, automatically, before the rest of your income becomes available for anything else. This is the single most important structural change most people can make to their financial behavior.

Build your emergency fund. If you do not have one, start one today. The first goal is $1,000. The ultimate goal is three to six months of essential living expenses, held in a separate, liquid, high-yield savings account that is never touched for anything other than a genuine emergency.

Establish a consistent saving rate. Even if it is small. Ten percent of your income is a strong starting target. Five percent is a meaningful beginning if ten isn't currently possible. The percentage matters less than the consistency - what you do every month, without exception, is what builds the foundation.

Separate your savings by purpose. Your emergency fund is not the same as your short-term savings for a planned expense, which is not the same as your long-term investment account. Keeping them separate — in clearly labeled, distinct accounts - prevents money designated for one purpose from being quietly consumed by another.

AREA 3: CREDIT

Your credit profile is being built whether you are participating in the building or not. Participation - deliberate, informed, consistent - is always better than absence.

Know your credit score. Check it through a free service such as Credit Karma, or through your bank if it offers that feature. Know what it is today, and understand what is driving it - positively and negatively.

Pull your full credit report. Visit AnnualCreditReport.com and review your complete report from all three major bureaus - Equifax, Experian, and TransUnion. Look for errors, inaccuracies, or accounts you don't recognize. Dispute anything that is incorrect through the bureau's formal dispute process.

Pay on time, every time. If this requires automation, automate it. Set up automatic minimum payments on every account so that a missed payment is never the result of forgetting. Then pay more than the minimum whenever possible.

Keep utilization low. Use no more than 30% of your available credit at any given time. Lower is better. The control that low utilization signals is a significant factor in building a strong profile.

Don't open accounts you don't need. Every application generates a hard inquiry. Every new account reduces the average age of your credit history. Open accounts with purpose, not convenience.

Never close your oldest account. Unless there is a compelling reason - an annual fee that can't be justified, for example - keeping your oldest account open maintains the length of your credit history, which works in your favor over time.

AREA 4: DEBT

Debt is not inherently destructive. Debt without a plan is. Every obligation you carry should be understood specifically and managed deliberately.

Know exactly what you owe. Every account. Every balance. Every interest rate. Every minimum payment. Write it down. The complete picture - seen clearly - is the beginning of being able to address it effectively.

Choose a repayment strategy and follow it. The avalanche method - highest interest rate first - minimizes total interest paid. The snowball method - smallest balance first - creates early momentum. Either works. Neither works without consistency.

Pay more than the minimum whenever possible. Minimum payments are designed to extend debt and maximize interest income for the lender. Even a small amount above the minimum compresses the timeline and reduces the total cost significantly.

Stop adding to what you are trying to reduce. Debt repayment without spending correction is a holding pattern. Address both simultaneously.

If you have student loans, know your options. Log in to StudentAid.gov. Know your balance, your servicer, your current repayment plan, and every alternative plan available to you. If you believe you may qualify for Public Service Loan Forgiveness or any other forgiveness program, research the requirements now and begin the certification process as early as possible.

AREA 5: INVESTING AND RETIREMENT

Saving preserves. Investing grows. Both are necessary, and neither replaces the other.

Open a retirement account if you don't have one. If your employer offers a 401(k) with a match, contribute at least enough to capture the full match - that match is part of your compensation, and not taking it is leaving money on the table. If your employer does not offer a retirement plan, open a Roth IRA through Fidelity, Vanguard, or Schwab. Contribute what you can. Increase the contribution as your income grows.

Understand what you are invested in. If your retirement account is sitting in a default money market fund or a low-yield savings vehicle, it is not growing the way a long-term investment account should. Research target-date funds or low-cost index funds as broadly diversified, low-maintenance options appropriate for most investors at this stage of life.

Automate your contributions. Recurring, automatic contributions remove the decision from the moment and make consistent investing the default rather than the deliberate choice.

Leave it alone. Market fluctuations are normal. Panic-selling during downturns converts paper losses into real ones and removes your money from the recovery that historically follows. Long-term investing requires long-term staying power. Build it and let time work.

If you are self-employed, research your options. A SEP-IRA or Solo 401(k) may allow significantly higher contributions than a standard IRA. Understanding which fits your situation and opening one is among the highest-impact financial actions available to someone who earns independently.

AREA 6: TAXES

Taxes are not optional and they are not a surprise - unless you treat them as one.

Understand how your income is taxed. If you receive a W-2, review your withholding to make sure the right amount is being deducted. If you earn any independent income, understand that you are responsible for setting aside your own tax obligation - typically 25% to 30% of every payment - and making quarterly estimated payments to the IRS.

Keep organized records. Track your income and deductible expenses throughout the year, not just at tax time. The more organized your records, the less stressful and more accurate your tax filing will be.

Understand the deductions available to you. The standard deduction, retirement account contributions, self-employment expenses - these reduce your taxable income and lower your tax bill. Knowing what applies to your situation is worth the time it takes to learn.

Work with a qualified tax professional when your situation warrants it. As your income grows and your financial life becomes more complex, professional guidance pays for itself in reduced errors, captured deductions, and strategic planning.

AREA 7: PROTECTION

What you build is only as valuable as the protection you put around it. Unprotected progress can be undone by a single unexpected event.

Have health insurance. If it is available through an employer, enroll. If not, explore options through HealthCare.gov or a private insurer. This is non-negotiable. A single uninsured medical event can produce financial damage that takes years to recover from.

Have renters insurance if you rent. It typically costs between $15 and $30 per month and covers your personal belongings against theft, fire, and other covered events. There is almost no scenario in which this cost is not worth paying.

Understand your disability insurance situation. Your ability to earn is your most valuable financial asset. If you became unable to work, how long could you sustain your financial obligations? If the answer is weeks rather than months, disability coverage deserves serious attention.

Consider life insurance if others depend on your income. If you have dependents - a partner who relies on your income, children, family members you support - term life insurance is straightforward, affordable when purchased young and healthy, and an important protection for the people who would be financially affected by your absence.

Review your coverage periodically. Your insurance needs change as your life does. What was appropriate at 22 may be insufficient at 28. A periodic review - annually, or whenever a significant life change occurs - ensures that your protection keeps pace with what you are building.

AREA 8: ENVIRONMENT AND MINDSET

The external and internal conditions of your financial life shape your decisions as powerfully as any specific strategy.

Be intentional about your environment. The people you spend the most time with, the content you consume regularly, and the standards you absorb from both will influence your financial behavior whether you choose that influence or not. Choose it deliberately.

Watch for lifestyle creep. Every income increase is an opportunity to strengthen your foundation - not just to expand your lifestyle. Commit in advance to directing a portion of every raise and bonus toward saving and investing before adjusting your spending.

Practice the pause. Before any non-essential purchase above a threshold you set for yourself, wait. Give your judgment time to participate in the decision. What survives the waiting period is genuinely wanted. What doesn't was impulse.

Build systems, not just intentions. Automate what can be automated. Create structures that make the right financial behaviors the default rather than the deliberate. The behaviors that run automatically are the ones that build consistently - regardless of motivation, energy, or the friction of any given day.

Review your progress regularly. Not obsessively. But consistently. A monthly financial review - thirty minutes to look at where you are relative to where you want to be - keeps the trajectory visible and makes course corrections possible before drift becomes damage.

YOUR STARTING POINT

Looking at this list, you may feel one of two things.

You may feel overwhelmed - like the distance between where you are and where this list describes is too large to close without an effort that feels beyond what you can currently manage.

Or you may feel motivated - energized by the clarity of seeing exactly what needs to be done, ready to begin immediately across every area simultaneously.

Neither of those responses, by itself, is useful.

The useful response is simpler and less dramatic than either.

Pick one thing.

Not the most important thing, necessarily. Not the thing that will make the biggest eventual difference. Just one thing - one area where you are not yet where you need to be, one action that is genuinely completable this week, one step that moves something from pending to in progress.

Take that step.

Then come back to the list.

Pick the next thing.

Take that step.

And keep going.

Because the checklist is not meant to be completed in a day. It is meant to be worked through over time - addressed steadily, revisited periodically, updated as your situation evolves and your financial life grows in complexity and strength.

The goal is not to finish the list.

The goal is to always be working on something on it.

Always moving. Always building. Always one step further along than you were the week before.

That movement - sustained, imperfect, consistent - is what builds the financial life that most people wish they had built earlier.

And you are building it now.

Not later.
Not when you feel ready.
Not when the amount feels significant or the plan feels complete or the timing feels right.

Now.
With what you have.
From where you are.

Your Action This Week: Go through the checklist above and mark every item honestly - completed, in progress, or not yet started. Don't filter toward what you wish were true. Mark what is actually true. Then identify the three most important items in the "not yet started" category - the three that, if addressed, would make the most meaningful difference to your financial position in the next twelve months. Choose one of those three to begin this week. Schedule specific time to work on it. Tell someone what you are committing to, if that helps you follow through. And then begin.

Not when you finish this book.

Now.

FINAL THOUGHTS

THE LIFE YOU DON'T HAVE TO FIX LATER

There is a conversation that happens quietly, in the minds of people who have lived long enough to see where their decisions led.

It doesn't happen at a specific age. It doesn't arrive on a schedule. It comes whenever someone looks honestly at the life they are living and measures it against the life they intended to build - and finds a gap between the two that they cannot fully explain by circumstance or bad luck alone.

In that moment, the thought is almost always the same.

I wish I had known this earlier.

Not - I wish I had earned more. Not - I wish I had been smarter or luckier or born into different circumstances. Those thoughts exist too, but they are not the most common one. The most common one is about timing. About the understanding that arrived too late to change the habits that were already formed, the patterns that were already entrenched, the consequences that were already compounding.

I wish I had known this earlier.

This book was written so that you don't have to think that thought.

Not because the information in these pages is secret or inaccessible - it isn't. Everything written here is available somewhere, to anyone willing to look for it. The problem has never been the availability of financial knowledge. The problem has always been the timing of its arrival - coming after the habits were established rather than before, after the patterns were running rather than in time to redirect them, after the cost of not knowing had already been paid rather than in time to avoid it.

That is the gap this book exists to close.

Not by overwhelming you with complexity. Not by turning personal finance into something that requires expertise to navigate. By giving you, as early as possible, the foundational understanding that allows you to move through your financial life with awareness rather than assumption - to make decisions that serve your future rather than decisions that simply respond to your present.

David was 40 when he sat down and took the kind of honest inventory that most people avoid for exactly as long as they can.

He looked at the areas of his financial life where he had paid attention early - where understanding had arrived before the stakes got high, where habits had been built before the pressure arrived to force them. The credit he had managed carefully since his mid-twenties. The retirement contributions he had started small and increased consistently. The emergency fund that had absorbed situations that would otherwise have required years of credit card debt to recover from. The insurance he had put in place before he ever needed it.

In those areas, his financial life felt solid. Not perfect - but solid. Built on a foundation that had been laid deliberately, over time, before it was required by circumstance.

Then he looked at the areas where understanding had arrived late. Where the habits hadn't been built until the consequences of not having them had already appeared. Where the cost of delay - in real dollars, in real stress, in real years of effort to correct what could have been built instead - was visible and specific and impossible to dismiss.

The contrast was clarifying in a way that no abstract principle could be.

The earlier he had started something, the easier it had become. The later he had started, the harder it had required.

Not because the actions themselves were different. Because the time available to them was.

That contrast - between the ease of building early and the difficulty of correcting late - is the central argument of everything in this book.

It is not an argument for perfection. Nothing in these pages has asked you to be perfect, to make every right decision, to navigate your financial life without error or detour or the occasional significant mistake. None of that is realistic, and none of it is the point.

The point is direction.

The point is that small, consistent actions taken in the right direction - begun early enough to compound, maintained consistently enough to build, applied broadly enough to cover the areas that actually shape financial outcomes - produce a life that is fundamentally different from the one produced by default patterns running without examination.

Not dramatically different in any single moment. Profoundly different over time.

That difference is the life you don't have to fix later.

Throughout this book, you have covered the terrain that shapes most people's financial reality - often without their full awareness.

You have seen how money works, and why earning it is only the beginning of the conversation. How credit is built, and why the habits established at the beginning of a credit history tend to define it for years. How saving functions not as restriction but as the structural foundation that makes everything else more stable.

How investing - started small, maintained consistently, given time - produces results that feel disproportionate to the effort involved. How taxes work whether you understand them or not, and why understanding them changes how much of your own money you actually keep. How insurance protects what you are building from the unpredictability that life delivers without permission.

You have seen how major decisions - buying a home, choosing a partner, taking on debt, structuring your income - carry longer consequences than they appear to in the moments they are made.

How the people around you influence your financial behavior in ways that are easy to underestimate and important to manage deliberately. How lifestyle creep converts income growth into lifestyle expansion rather than financial foundation growth, silently and without announcement. How emergency funds transform unexpected events from crises into problems. How debt accumulates through decisions that seem reasonable individually and costly collectively.

You have seen how consistency, applied over time, builds more than any single dramatic action could. How delayed gratification - the willingness to choose later over now, not always but consistently enough - is one of the clearest predictors of financial outcomes over a lifetime. How discipline built into systems outlasts and outperforms motivation dependent on feeling. How the cost of waiting is real, specific, and compounding - and how starting, even imperfectly, is always worth more than continuing to wait for the conditions that make starting feel fully justified.

And you have seen, finally, what becomes possible when these things are understood and applied early enough to compound - the life of stability, flexibility, and genuine financial control that is available to anyone willing to begin and willing to continue.

That life does not require exceptional income. It does not require extraordinary discipline or sophisticated financial knowledge or a perfect plan executed without error. It requires something simpler and more accessible than any of those things.

It requires awareness - of how the systems around you work, of how your decisions connect to your outcomes, of where your current habits are actually taking you.

It requires intention - the willingness to direct your financial life rather than simply live inside whatever it becomes by default.

It requires consistency - not the consistency of perfection, but the consistency of continuation. Of resuming when you have stopped. Of maintaining when maintaining is less exciting than starting. Of trusting the process through the long, flat stretches before the results become visible.

And it requires starting - not when conditions are ideal, not when the plan is complete, not when the amount feels significant or the timing feels right. Starting from exactly where you are, with exactly what you currently understand, with whatever is available to you right now.

Those things - awareness, intention, consistency, and starting - are not financial strategies. They are decisions about how to move through the world. And they are decisions that are available to you regardless of your income, your current financial position, your past mistakes, or the distance between where you are and where you want to be.

There are two futures available to you from this point.
In one of them, this book becomes another thing you engaged with, absorbed in principle, and then set aside without meaningfully changing the behaviors it described. The knowledge stays. The habits don't change. The patterns continue running in the same direction they were running before you started reading.

And at some point - five years from now, ten years, twenty - you sit with the quiet, honest inventory that David sat with, and you find the gap between what was possible and what was built.

In the other, something shifts. Not dramatically - not a complete transformation of everything at once. But something shifts. One habit changes. One system gets built. One area that was being ignored gets addressed. And from that one change, momentum builds. Another habit follows. Another area gets addressed. The pattern of your financial life - gradually, almost imperceptibly, but genuinely - bends in a different direction.

And over time, that different direction becomes a different destination.

A life with a foundation beneath it. A life where the unexpected is manageable rather than devastating. A life where money is a tool you direct rather than a force that directs you. A life where the decisions available to you are genuinely choices rather than constraints imposed by the accumulation of what wasn't built.

The life you don't have to fix later.

That future is built from what you do next.

Not from what you intend. Not from what you understand. From what you actually do - specifically, consistently, starting as soon as possible and continuing long after the starting feels difficult.

So close this book with something more than the understanding you started it with.

Close it with a decision.

One specific, concrete, immediately actionable decision about one thing you will do differently starting this week.

Not ten things. One.

Write it down. Make it specific. Give it a timeline. And then honor it - not because the single action will transform your financial life, but because the single action is how every financial life that was ever transformed actually began.

One step. Then another. Then another.

Repeated over time.

Building something that no single step could have built alone.
Because this is how it works.
Not in the dramatic moments.
In the ordinary ones.

The week you opened the savings account. The month you pulled your credit report for the first time and actually read it. The year you started the retirement contributions you had been meaning to start. The decision you made, quietly and without fanfare, to direct your money rather than simply spend it.

Those moments - unremarkable in the instant they occurred, significant in their accumulation - are the moments that build the life.

Your life.

The one you are building right now.
Whether you are paying attention to it or not.
Pay attention to it.
Direct it.

Build it with intention, with consistency, and with the understanding that what you do while you are still young will echo through everything that comes after.

You don't get this time back.
But you have it now.

Use it.

Because the life you don't have to fix later -
is the life you start building today.

Thank you for reading. Now go do something with it.

RESOURCES

The information in this book is designed to give you a strong foundation - but a foundation is only the beginning. The tools, websites, and books listed here are the next step. They will help you apply what you've learned, go deeper in the areas that matter most to your situation, and stay informed as your financial life grows in complexity.

Everything listed here is either free or widely accessible. None of it requires a financial background to use effectively. Start with what is most relevant to where you currently are, and build from there.

TOOLS AND WEBSITES

Credit and Credit Reports

AnnualCreditReport.com The only federally mandated source for free credit reports from all three major bureaus - Equifax, Experian, and TransUnion. You are entitled to one free report from each bureau per year. Use it. Review every report carefully for errors, inaccuracies, and accounts you don't recognize.

Credit Karma (creditkarma.com) Free credit score monitoring with regular updates and explanations of the factors affecting your score. Useful for tracking your credit profile over time and catching changes quickly.

Experian (experian.com) In addition to credit report access, Experian offers free credit monitoring and tools for understanding and improving your credit profile.

Budgeting and Spending

YNAB — You Need A Budget (youneedabudget.com) One of the most effective budgeting tools available, built around the principle of giving every dollar a job before it is spent. Subscription-based, but widely regarded as worth the cost for the financial clarity it creates.

Mint (mint.com) Free budgeting and expense tracking tool that connects to your accounts and categorizes your spending automatically. Useful for getting a clear picture of where your money is actually going.

EveryDollar (everydollar.com) A straightforward zero-based budgeting app built on the principle that every dollar of income is assigned a purpose before the month begins. Free version available, with a premium option for automatic bank syncing.

Saving and Banking

High-Yield Savings Accounts Online banks consistently offer significantly higher interest rates on savings accounts than traditional brick-and-mortar banks. Institutions worth researching include Ally Bank, Marcus by Goldman Sachs, Discover Bank, and SoFi. Rates change regularly - search "best high-yield savings accounts" for current comparisons before opening one.

Bankrate (bankrate.com) Independent comparisons of savings account rates, CD rates, and other financial products. Useful for finding the most competitive options currently available without bias toward any specific institution.

Investing and Retirement

Fidelity (fidelity.com) One of the largest and most reputable investment brokerages, offering Roth IRAs, traditional IRAs, and brokerage accounts with no account minimums, no annual fees, and a strong selection of low-cost index funds. An excellent starting point for most people opening their first investment account.

Vanguard (vanguard.com) The brokerage most associated with low-cost index fund investing. Vanguard pioneered the index fund concept and remains one of the most trusted institutions for long-term, passive investing. Particularly strong for retirement account management.

Schwab (schwab.com) Another major, reputable brokerage with no account minimums, commission-free trades, and a wide range of investment options. Strong educational resources for newer investors.

Investor.gov The U.S. Securities and Exchange Commission's investor education website. Free, unbiased information on investing basics, compound interest calculators, and tools for understanding how investment growth works over time. The compound interest calculator here is particularly worth using - seeing the numbers is more motivating than reading about them.

Retirement Planning Specific

IRS.gov - Retirement Plans Official IRS guidance on contribution limits, eligibility requirements, and rules governing IRAs, 401(k)s, SEP-IRAs, and Solo 401(k)s. Updated annually when limits change.

SmartAsset Retirement Calculator (smartasset.com) Free tool for modeling retirement savings growth based on your current age, contribution amount, expected return, and target retirement age. Useful for understanding how much starting earlier - or later - actually changes the outcome.

Student Loans

StudentAid.gov The official U.S. Department of Education website for federal student loan management. Log in to see your complete loan summary, current repayment plan, servicer information, and available repayment alternatives. The Loan Simulator tool allows you to compare repayment plans side by side and model the impact of different strategies on your total cost and monthly payment.

National Foundation for Credit Counseling (nfcc.org) Nonprofit organization offering free and low-cost financial counseling, including student loan guidance and debt management support. If your student loan or debt situation feels genuinely unmanageable, a certified nonprofit credit counselor is a far better resource than any for-profit debt settlement company.

Taxes

IRS.gov The authoritative source for all federal tax information - filing requirements, estimated quarterly payment schedules, deduction guidance, and free filing options. The IRS Free File program allows eligible taxpayers to file federal returns at no cost through participating software providers.

IRS Free File (irs.gov/filing/free-file-do-your-federal-taxes-for-free) If your income falls below a certain threshold — currently $79,000 or below — you may qualify to file your federal taxes for free through IRS-partnered software. Check the current eligibility requirements each filing season.

IRS Withholding Estimator (irs.gov/individuals/tax-withholding-estimator) Free tool for calculating whether your current withholding is appropriate for your situation. Particularly useful after a raise, a job change, or any other significant income shift.

Insurance

HealthCare.gov The federal health insurance marketplace, where individuals and families can compare and enroll in health insurance plans. Open enrollment occurs annually, with special enrollment periods available for qualifying life events such as job loss, marriage, or the birth of a child. Income-based subsidies are available and can significantly reduce premiums for eligible individuals.

Healthcare.gov - Medicaid and CHIP If your income falls below certain thresholds, you may qualify for Medicaid or the Children's Health Insurance Program at little or no cost. Eligibility varies by state.

NAIC (naic.org) - National Association of Insurance Commissioners Free resource for understanding different types of insurance, comparing providers, and verifying that an insurance company is licensed in your state.

General Financial Education

Consumer Financial Protection Bureau (cfpb.gov) One of the most comprehensive free financial education resources available. The CFPB offers clear, unbiased guidance on credit, debt, mortgages, student loans, and virtually every other aspect of personal finance. Particularly useful for understanding your rights as a consumer and for navigating financial disputes.

MyMoney.gov The U.S. government's official financial literacy website, developed by the Financial Literacy and Education Commission. Covers budgeting, saving, investing, credit, and more.

Khan Academy — Personal Finance (khanacademy.org) Free, structured video-based courses on personal finance fundamentals. Clear, accessible, and genuinely educational. A strong resource for anyone who wants to go deeper on any of the topics covered in this book.

RECOMMENDED READING

The books below were selected for their lasting relevance to the principles covered in this book. Each one goes deeper on a dimension of personal finance that a single chapter can only introduce. As with any resource list, newer titles may have emerged since this was written - treat this as a starting point, not a complete inventory.

I Will Teach You to Be Rich - Ramit Sethi Practical, direct, and written specifically for young adults navigating financial decisions for the first time. Covers banking, credit, investing, and budgeting in a voice that is accessible without being condescending. Particularly strong on automation and building systems that make good financial behavior the default rather than the deliberate choice. One of the most useful personal finance books written for people in their twenties who find traditional financial advice dry or disconnected from their actual lives.

The Psychology of Money - Morgan Housel One of the most readable and insightful books written on the behavioral dimensions of financial decision-making. Explores why people make the financial choices they do, why intelligent people consistently make poor financial decisions, and why behavior matters more than knowledge in determining long-term financial outcomes. Essential reading for anyone who has absorbed good financial advice and still struggles to apply it consistently. The answer to why that gap exists is in this book.

The Millionaire Next Door - Thomas J. Stanley and William D. Danko A research-based examination of the actual behaviors and characteristics of wealthy Americans - most of whom, the data reveals, live significantly below their means, build wealth through decades of consistent saving, and bear little resemblance to the cultural image of financial success. A powerful and lasting antidote to the equation of high income with financial security. Changes fundamentally how you see wealth and who actually has it.

Your Money or Your Life - Vicki Robin and Joe Dominguez A values-based approach to personal finance that asks a more foundational question than most financial books: what is money actually for, and is the way you are earning and spending it aligned with what you genuinely care about? Particularly valuable for anyone who feels financially functional but somehow still unsatisfied — and wants to understand the deeper reason why. Reframes the relationship between money, time, and the life you are actually trying to build.

Broke Millennial - Erin Lowry Written specifically for young adults who feel overwhelmed by personal finance and don't know where to begin. Conversational, non-judgmental, and genuinely practical. Covers budgeting, debt, and the financial conversations most people avoid in a voice that meets the reader exactly where they are. An excellent companion to this book for anyone who wants a second perspective on the fundamentals in a similarly accessible format.

A Random Walk Down Wall Street - Burton Malkiel The definitive, research-based case for passive, index-fund investing over active stock selection or market timing. Rigorous and thoroughly argued, but accessible to a non-expert reader willing to engage with the evidence. Essential reading for anyone who wants to understand in depth why the simple, consistent investing approach described in this book outperforms more active strategies the vast majority of the time - and why that finding is far more durable than most people realize.

The Total Money Makeover - Dave Ramsey A step-by-step framework for eliminating debt and building financial stability, structured around a sequential set of steps that move from emergency fund to debt payoff to investing. Particularly useful for anyone carrying significant debt who needs a clear, ordered plan to work through rather than a set of general principles to apply independently. The approach is prescriptive and conservative - some readers find the structure highly motivating, others prefer more flexibility. Worth reading for the debt elimination framework regardless of where you land on its broader philosophy.

A NOTE ON USING THESE RESOURCES

No resource on this list will change your financial life by itself. Information without application is simply information. What changes financial lives is the combination of understanding and consistent action - and that combination is something only you can create.

Use these tools and books the same way you should use this book: not as a substitute for doing the work, but as support for doing it better. Start with the one most relevant to where you are right now. Apply what you find before moving to the next one. Let your understanding build in layers, grounded in action rather than accumulation.

Because the goal was never to know more about personal finance.

The goal was always to build a better financial life.

These resources exist to help you do exactly that.

GLOSSARY OF KEY FINANCIAL TERMS

The terms below appear throughout this book and throughout financial life in general. Understanding them clearly — not just approximately - is part of the foundational awareness that makes every other financial decision easier. This glossary is not exhaustive. It is practical. These are the terms you are most likely to encounter in the situations this book prepares you for.

401(k) An employer-sponsored retirement savings account that allows employees to contribute a portion of their pre-tax income toward retirement. Many employers match a percentage of employee contributions - effectively adding free money to the account. Contributions and investment growth are tax-deferred, meaning taxes are paid when the money is withdrawn in retirement. Contribution limits are set by the IRS and adjusted periodically.

Annual Percentage Rate (APR) The yearly cost of borrowing money, expressed as a percentage. APR includes the interest rate plus any additional fees associated with the loan, making it a more complete measure of borrowing cost than the interest rate alone. When comparing credit cards or loans, APR is the most useful number to compare.

Asset Anything you own that has economic value - savings accounts, investment accounts, retirement accounts, real estate, vehicles, or any other property. In personal finance, assets are what you own, as opposed to liabilities, which are what you owe.

Avalanche Method A debt repayment strategy in which extra payments are directed toward the debt with the highest interest rate first, while minimum payments are maintained on all other debts. When the highest-rate debt is eliminated, payments are redirected to the next highest rate. Mathematically, this approach minimizes the total interest paid over the life of the debt.

Balance Transfer The process of moving an existing credit card balance to a new credit card, typically one offering a low or zero introductory interest rate for a defined promotional period. Can be an effective tool for reducing interest costs during debt repayment, provided the balance is paid off before the promotional rate expires.

Bankruptcy A legal process through which individuals or businesses who cannot repay their debts may seek relief from some or all of what they owe. Personal bankruptcy typically takes one of two forms - Chapter 7, which discharges most unsecured debts, and Chapter 13, which restructures debt into a repayment plan. Bankruptcy has significant and long-lasting consequences for credit history and should be considered only as a last resort after all other options have been exhausted.

Beneficiary A person designated to receive the assets of an account, insurance policy, or estate upon the account holder's death. Keeping beneficiary designations current on retirement accounts, life insurance policies, and other financial accounts is an important and frequently overlooked aspect of financial planning.

Budget A plan that allocates income toward specific categories of spending, saving, and debt repayment before that income is spent. A budget is not a restriction - it is a direction. It tells your money where to go before the moment of spending determines where it goes instead.

Capital Gain The profit realized from selling an asset - such as a stock, bond, or piece of real estate - for more than its purchase price. Capital gains may be subject to taxation, with the rate depending on how long the asset was held before being sold. Assets held for more than one year typically qualify for lower long-term capital gains tax rates.

Capitalization (of Interest) The process by which unpaid interest is added to the principal balance of a loan, after which interest begins accruing on the larger combined amount. Common with student loans during periods of deferment or when interest goes unpaid during school. Capitalization increases the total cost of the loan and the monthly payment under standard repayment.

Collateral An asset pledged by a borrower to secure a loan. If the borrower fails to repay the loan, the lender has the right to seize the collateral. A mortgage uses the home as collateral. An auto loan uses the vehicle. Loans secured by collateral typically carry lower interest rates than unsecured loans because the lender's risk is reduced.

Compound Interest Interest calculated on both the original principal and the interest previously accumulated. Often described as interest earning interest. Compounding is the mechanism that makes early investing so powerful - and high-interest debt so costly. Time is the most important variable in compound interest. The longer money has to compound, the more dramatic the effect.

Credit The ability to borrow money or access goods and services with the agreement to pay for them later. In a broader sense, credit refers to the system by which lenders evaluate the trustworthiness of borrowers based on their history of repaying obligations. Your credit history and credit score are the primary tools used to assess your creditworthiness.

Credit Bureau One of three major companies - Equifax, Experian, and TransUnion — that collect and maintain credit information on consumers. Lenders report your borrowing and repayment behavior to these bureaus, which use that information to generate your credit report and, in combination with scoring models, your credit score.

Credit Limit The maximum amount a lender permits a borrower to carry on a revolving credit account such as a credit card. Having a high credit limit does not mean the full amount should be used - keeping utilization well below the limit is an important factor in maintaining a strong credit profile.

Credit Report A detailed record of your credit history, maintained by the three major credit bureaus. Includes information on every credit account you have opened, your payment history on each, your current balances, any public records such as bankruptcies, and inquiries from lenders who have recently checked your credit. You are entitled to one free report from each bureau annually through AnnualCreditReport.com.

Credit Score A numerical summary of your credit history, typically ranging from 300 to 850 under the most widely used FICO scoring model. Higher scores indicate stronger creditworthiness and generally result in access to better interest rates and more favorable lending terms. The score is calculated based on payment history, credit utilization, length of credit history, credit mix, and recent inquiries.

Credit Utilization The percentage of your available revolving credit that you are currently using. Calculated by dividing your total credit card balances by your total credit limits. Keeping utilization below 30% is generally recommended for maintaining a strong credit profile.

Lower utilization signals financial control and is viewed positively by lenders.

Deductible In insurance, the amount you are required to pay out of pocket before your insurance coverage begins to pay. A higher deductible typically results in a lower monthly premium, and a lower deductible results in a higher premium. Choosing the right deductible requires balancing the monthly cost of the premium against your ability to cover the deductible amount if a claim becomes necessary.

Default The failure to repay a debt according to the agreed terms. On federal student loans, default occurs after 270 days of missed payments. Default has serious consequences including significant damage to credit, potential wage garnishment, and loss of eligibility for future federal financial aid. Options for avoiding default - including income-driven repayment and deferment - are far more favorable than the consequences of allowing default to occur.

Deferment A temporary period during which a borrower is not required to make payments on a loan, typically granted during specific circumstances such as enrollment in school, unemployment, or economic hardship. Interest may or may not continue to accrue during deferment depending on the type of loan.

Depreciation The reduction in value of an asset over time. Vehicles depreciate rapidly - a new car typically loses a significant percentage of its value within the first few years of ownership. Understanding depreciation is relevant to major purchase decisions, particularly when weighing the cost of new versus used assets.

Discretionary Income The portion of your income remaining after essential expenses - housing, food, transportation, utilities, and minimum debt payments - have been paid. Discretionary income is what is available for savings, investments, non-essential spending, and additional debt repayment. In the context of student loan repayment, discretionary income has a specific federal definition used to calculate payments under income-driven repayment plans.

Diversification The practice of spreading investments across multiple asset types, sectors, or geographies to reduce the risk that any single investment's poor performance significantly damages the overall portfolio. Index funds provide built-in diversification by holding small positions in a large number of companies simultaneously.

Dividend A portion of a company's profits distributed to shareholders, typically on a quarterly basis. Dividends can be received as cash or reinvested to purchase additional shares. Dividend-paying investments can provide a stream of income in addition to potential price appreciation.

Emergency Fund Money set aside specifically to cover unexpected, necessary expenses - job loss, medical situations, critical car or home repairs - without requiring the use of credit or other borrowing. A fully funded emergency fund typically covers three to six months of essential living expenses and is held in a liquid, accessible savings account separate from everyday spending accounts.

Equity The portion of an asset's value that you own outright, as opposed to what is owed on it. In homeownership, equity is the difference between the market value of the home and the outstanding mortgage balance. Equity grows as the mortgage is paid down and as the property value increases. Building equity is one of the primary financial arguments for homeownership over renting.

Expense Ratio The annual fee charged by a mutual fund or exchange-traded fund, expressed as a percentage of the assets invested. A fund with an expense ratio of 0.05% charges fifty cents per year for every $1,000 invested. Low expense ratios - characteristic of index funds offered through major brokerages - are an important factor in long-term investment returns because fees compound just as returns do, working against the investor over time.

FICO Score The most widely used credit scoring model, developed by the Fair Isaac Corporation. Scores range from 300 to 850 and are calculated based on five factors: payment history, credit utilization, length of credit history, credit mix, and new inquiries. Most lenders use FICO scores to evaluate creditworthiness, though the specific version of the FICO model used may vary by lender and loan type.

Forbearance A temporary reduction or suspension of loan payments, granted by the lender during periods of financial hardship. Unlike deferment, interest typically continues to accrue on all loan types during forbearance. Forbearance is a tool for managing temporary financial difficulty - it does not reduce what is owed and may increase the total cost of the loan if interest capitalizes at the end of the forbearance period.

Gross Income Total income earned before any deductions - taxes, retirement contributions, insurance premiums, or other withholdings. Gross income is what you earn. Net income is what you actually receive. Financial planning and budgeting should be based on net income, not gross.

Hard Inquiry A review of your credit report initiated by a lender when you apply for new credit. Hard inquiries are recorded on your credit report and can temporarily lower your credit score. Multiple hard inquiries within a short period can signal financial instability to lenders. Rate shopping for mortgages or auto loans within a defined window is typically treated as a single inquiry by most scoring models.

Index Fund A type of investment fund designed to replicate the performance of a specific market index - such as the S&P 500, which tracks the 500 largest publicly traded U.S. companies. Index funds provide broad diversification, typically carry very low expense ratios, and have historically outperformed the majority of actively managed funds over long time periods. Widely recommended for beginning investors and for long-term retirement accounts.

Individual Retirement Account (IRA) A personal retirement savings account that offers tax advantages to encourage long-term saving. The two most common types are the Traditional IRA, which allows pre-tax contributions and taxes withdrawals in retirement, and the Roth IRA, which uses after-tax contributions and allows tax-free growth and withdrawals. Contribution limits and income eligibility requirements are set by the IRS and adjusted periodically.

Inflation The rate at which the general level of prices for goods and services rises over time, reducing the purchasing power of money. A dollar today buys less than a dollar did ten years ago because of inflation. Investing - rather than simply saving - is important in part because investment returns, over time, have historically outpaced inflation, preserving and growing the real value of money.

Interest Rate The cost of borrowing money or the return earned on money saved or invested, expressed as a percentage. On debt, a higher interest rate means borrowing costs more. On savings and investments, a higher rate means money grows faster. Understanding interest rates - and the difference between them across various financial products - is foundational to making informed decisions about both borrowing and saving.

Liability A financial obligation - money you owe to another party. Credit card balances, student loans, car loans, and mortgages are all liabilities. In personal finance, net worth is calculated by subtracting total liabilities from total assets.

Lifecycle Fund (Target-Date Fund) A type of investment fund designed to automatically adjust its asset allocation over time as the investor approaches a target retirement date. Typically holds a higher proportion of stocks when the target date is far away and gradually shifts toward more conservative, bond-heavy allocations as the date approaches. A straightforward, low-maintenance option for retirement investors who prefer not to actively manage their allocation.

Liquidity The ease with which an asset can be converted to cash without significant loss of value. A savings account is highly liquid - funds are accessible immediately. Real estate is illiquid - converting it to cash requires time, effort, and transaction costs. Emergency funds should be held in highly liquid accounts to ensure accessibility when unexpected situations arise.

Minimum Payment The smallest amount a borrower is required to pay on a revolving credit account each billing cycle to keep the account in good standing. Paying only the minimum on a high-balance account results in very slow principal reduction and significant interest accumulation over time. Minimum payments are designed to extend the life of the debt and maximize interest income for the lender.

Net Income Income remaining after all deductions - taxes, retirement contributions, insurance, and other withholdings - have been subtracted from gross income. Net income is the amount actually deposited into your account and the number on which realistic budgeting and financial planning should be based.

Net Worth The difference between everything you own - your assets - and everything you owe - your liabilities. Net worth is the most comprehensive single measure of financial position. A positive net worth means assets exceed liabilities. A negative net worth means liabilities exceed assets. Tracking net worth over time is one of the most useful ways to measure overall financial progress.

Overdraft Occurs when a transaction causes an account balance to fall below zero. Banks may cover the transaction and charge an overdraft fee, or decline the transaction. Overdraft fees are typically significant relative to the amounts involved and can accumulate quickly. Setting up low-balance alerts and maintaining a buffer in your checking account are simple ways to avoid them.

Principal The original amount borrowed on a loan or the original amount deposited or invested, before interest is added or earned. On a loan, the principal is the balance on which interest is calculated. As payments are made, the principal decreases. Understanding how much of each payment goes toward principal versus interest — especially in the early years of a loan - is important for evaluating the true cost of borrowing.

Private Mortgage Insurance (PMI) Insurance required by most lenders when a home buyer makes a down payment of less than 20% of the purchase price. PMI protects the lender - not the borrower - against the risk of default. It adds a monthly cost to the mortgage payment and provides no direct benefit to the homeowner. PMI can typically be removed once the homeowner has built sufficient equity, usually when the loan balance reaches 80% of the home's value.

Public Service Loan Forgiveness (PSLF) A federal program that forgives the remaining balance of federal student loans for borrowers who work full-time for qualifying government or nonprofit employers and make 120 qualifying payments under an income-driven repayment plan. Forgiveness under PSLF is tax-free. Requires precise adherence to program requirements - employment certification should be submitted annually from the beginning of qualifying employment.

Refinancing The process of replacing an existing loan with a new one, typically at a different interest rate or with different terms. Can reduce monthly payments, lower the total cost of borrowing, or both - depending on the new rate and terms relative to the original loan. Refinancing federal student loans into a private loan permanently eliminates access to federal protections and forgiveness programs.

Roth IRA A type of individual retirement account funded with after-tax dollars. Contributions are not tax-deductible, but investment growth and qualified withdrawals in retirement are entirely tax-free. Generally considered the stronger choice for young people who expect their income - and therefore their tax rate - to increase over time. Contribution limits and income eligibility requirements are set by the IRS and adjusted periodically.

SEP-IRA (Simplified Employee Pension) A retirement savings account designed for self-employed individuals and small business owners. Allows significantly higher annual contributions than a standard IRA - up to 25% of net self-employment income, subject to an annual cap set by the IRS. Contributions are tax-deductible. A straightforward and powerful retirement savings vehicle for those who earn income independently.

Snowball Method A debt repayment strategy in which extra payments are directed toward the debt with the smallest balance first, while minimum payments are maintained on all others. When the smallest balance is eliminated, payments are redirected to the next smallest. Creates early wins that build psychological momentum. Costs more in total interest than the avalanche method but may be more motivating for some borrowers.

Soft Inquiry A review of your credit report that does not affect your credit score. Soft inquiries occur when you check your own credit, when a company checks your credit for pre-approval offers, or when an employer conducts a background check. Unlike hard inquiries, soft inquiries are not visible to lenders and have no impact on creditworthiness assessments.

Solo 401(k) A retirement savings account designed for self-employed individuals with no employees other than a spouse. Allows contributions both as the employee and as the employer, resulting in significantly higher potential contribution limits than a standard IRA or SEP-

IRA. A strong option for self-employed individuals with growing income who want to maximize retirement savings.

Tax Bracket One of several income ranges established by the IRS, each associated with a specific marginal tax rate. The U.S. uses a progressive tax system, meaning different portions of your income are taxed at different rates. Only the income within each bracket is taxed at that bracket's rate - not your entire income. Understanding how tax brackets work prevents the common misconception that earning more money can result in taking home less.

Tax Deduction An expense that reduces your taxable income, thereby lowering the amount of tax owed. Common deductions include retirement account contributions, student loan interest, and - for self-employed individuals - qualifying business expenses. The standard deduction is available to all taxpayers and reduces taxable income by a fixed amount set annually by the IRS.

Term Life Insurance A type of life insurance that provides coverage for a specific period - typically 10, 20, or 30 years - at a fixed monthly or annual premium. If the insured person dies during the term, the policy pays a death benefit to the designated beneficiaries. Term policies are significantly more affordable than permanent life insurance products and provide the core protection most people need without unnecessary complexity.

Vesting The process by which an employee gains ownership of employer contributions to a retirement account over time. An employer may contribute to your 401(k) but require you to remain employed for a defined period before those contributions are fully yours. Understanding the vesting schedule of any employer match is important - leaving a job before fully vesting may result in forfeiting some or all of the employer's contributions.

W-2 A tax form provided by employers to employees at the end of each calendar year, summarizing total wages earned and taxes withheld during the year. Used to file federal and state income tax returns. If you work as an employee, you will receive a W-2. If you earn income as an independent contractor or self-employed individual, you will typically receive a 1099 instead.

W-4 A form completed by employees when beginning a new job that tells the employer how much federal income tax to withhold from each paycheck. Completing a W-4 accurately - and updating it when significant life changes occur - helps ensure that the right amount is withheld throughout the year, reducing the likelihood of a large tax bill or an unnecessarily large refund at filing time.

1099 A tax form used to report income received outside of traditional employment - including freelance work, contract income, self-employment income, and certain investment distributions. Unlike W-2 employees whose taxes are withheld by their employer, recipients of 1099 income are responsible for setting aside and paying their own taxes, including self-employment tax.

Financial terminology evolves and new terms emerge as financial products and regulations change. When you encounter a term not included here, the Consumer Financial Protection Bureau's online glossary at cfpb.gov is a reliable and current resource for clear, unbiased definitions.

YOUR ACTION CHECKLIST

WHAT TO DO WHILE YOU'RE STILL YOUNG

This checklist is a companion to the full book - a single reference page that brings together every key action into one place. Use it to assess where you currently stand, track your progress over time, and identify what to work on next.

You do not need to complete everything at once. You need to always be working on something.

Check off each item honestly - not based on what you intend to do, but based on what is actually in place.

SECTION 1: FOUNDATIONAL AWARENESS

- I know exactly how much income I receive each month, from every source, after taxes
- I have tracked every expense for at least one full month and know where my money is actually going
- I have calculated my net worth - total assets minus total liabilities - and written it down

- I review my income, expenses, and overall financial position at least once per month
- I have a written budget that assigns every dollar of income a purpose before it is spent

SECTION 2: SAVING

- I save a fixed percentage of my income before spending what remains — not after
- I have a dedicated emergency fund account, separate from my everyday spending account
- My emergency fund contains at least $1,000
- My emergency fund contains at least one month of essential living expenses
- My emergency fund contains three to six months of essential living expenses
- My savings transfers are automated - they happen without requiring a decision each month
- I have separate accounts for separate savings purposes - emergency fund, short-term goals, and long-term building

SECTION 3: CREDIT

- I know my current credit score
- I have pulled my full credit report from all three bureaus and reviewed it for errors
- I have disputed any inaccuracies on my credit report
- All of my credit accounts are paid on time, every month - with automatic payments set up where needed
- My credit utilization is consistently below 30% across all accounts
- I have at least one credit account open and actively managed
- I do not apply for new credit unless I have a specific and considered reason to do so

- My oldest credit account remains open and in good standing

SECTION 4: DEBT

- I know the exact balance, interest rate, and minimum payment for every debt I carry
- I have a written repayment strategy - avalanche or snowball - and I am following it consistently
- I am paying more than the minimum on at least one debt every month
- I am not adding new debt while actively working to reduce existing debt
- If I have student loans, I have logged in to StudentAid.gov and reviewed my full loan summary
- If I have student loans, I understand my current repayment plan and at least two alternatives
- If I may qualify for Public Service Loan Forgiveness, I have researched the requirements and begun the certification process

SECTION 5: INVESTING AND RETIREMENT

- I have a retirement account open and actively contributing to it
- If my employer offers a 401(k) match, I am contributing at least enough to capture the full match
- If I do not have an employer plan, I have opened a Roth IRA or Traditional IRA
- I understand what my retirement money is invested in and have confirmed it is in a broadly diversified, low-cost option
- My retirement contributions are automated - they recur without requiring a monthly decision
- If I am self-employed, I have researched and opened a SEP-IRA or Solo 401(k)

- I have used an online calculator to model what my current contributions will grow to by retirement

SECTION 6: TAXES

- I understand how my income is taxed - whether through employer withholding or self-managed quarterly payments
- If I earn any independent income, I am setting aside 25–30% of every payment for taxes before spending the rest
- If I earn independent income, I understand estimated quarterly tax payments and am making them on schedule
- I keep organized records of my income and deductible expenses throughout the year - not just at tax time
- I have reviewed my W-4 withholding to confirm the right amount is being deducted from each paycheck
- I understand which deductions apply to my situation and am taking advantage of them

SECTION 7: PROTECTION

- I have health insurance coverage currently in place
- I have renters insurance if I rent my home
- I understand what my auto insurance covers and have confirmed it is sufficient for my situation
- I have evaluated my disability insurance situation and understand what protection is in place if I become unable to work
- If others depend on my income, I have life insurance coverage in place
- I review my insurance coverage at least once per year or whenever a significant life change occurs

SECTION 8: MAJOR LIFE DECISIONS

- I have had honest, specific conversations about money with my partner - or have committed to doing so before combining finances
- I understand the full cost of homeownership - not just the mortgage - and have assessed my genuine readiness before considering a purchase
- I have evaluated my current environment honestly and am intentional about the people and content that influence my financial thinking and behavior
- I have a plan for what happens to my finances if my income decreases significantly or stops temporarily

SECTION 9: MINDSET AND HABITS

- My most important financial behaviors are automated or systematized - they run without depending on motivation
- I practice a waiting period before non-essential purchases above a threshold I have set for myself
- When my income increases, I direct a portion of that increase toward saving or investing before adjusting my lifestyle
- I conduct a monthly financial review - even briefly - to confirm my direction and catch drift before it becomes damage
- I have identified and am actively addressing the one financial area whose delay is currently costing me the most

WHERE TO FOCUS NEXT

Use this section after completing your first honest review of the checklist above.

Items I have fully addressed:

____

____

____

Items I am currently working on:

____

____

____

The one item I will begin this week:

____

The date I will review this checklist again:

____

This checklist is not a test. It is a map. You are not graded on how many boxes are checked today - you are measured by how many more are checked the next time you return to it. Come back to it every three to six months. Watch the map fill in. And keep going.

ABOUT THE AUTHOR

Alice Truman is a relationship educator, emotional wellness advocate, and storyteller with a passion for helping people build stronger, more meaningful lives-both in love and in life. She is especially committed to guiding young people as they step into adulthood, equipping them with the awareness, tools, and confidence needed to make decisions that support their future.

Her work is grounded in empathy, emotional intelligence, and the belief that real connection-whether with others or within oneself—begins where the armor ends.

Blending warmth, humor, and practical wisdom, Alice empowers readers to have honest conversations, break unhealthy patterns, and approach life with clarity and courage. She believes relationships and life outcomes don't thrive on autopilot-they grow through presence, intention, and the willingness to show up, even when it's uncomfortable.

When she's not writing or teaching, Alice enjoys quiet mornings, meaningful conversations, and good coffee—preferably shared with someone she can laugh with and grow alongside.

ALSO BY ALICE TRUMAN

I'm Ready is a powerful guide for the woman who has it all together on the outside, but feels emotionally weary on the inside. Written with warmth, wisdom, and truth, this transformational book invites you to take off the emotional armor, release old patterns, and open yourself to the kind of love you truly desire - without abandoning your strength.

We Got This: In this refreshing and relatable relationship book, We Got This! serves up the essential "ingredients" that every lasting love needs. Blending wisdom, humor, and a dash of tough love, this guide is perfect for couples who want to strengthen their bond, reignite their connection, and learn how to truly serve the relationship - not just themselves.

Why Can't We Get Along?: Whether you're dating, married, or recovering from a breakup, Why Can't We Get Along? helps you understand why love feels so hard - and how to finally fix it. Packed with practical advice, emotional insight, and honest examples, this relationship guide will help you break the cycle of confusion, silence, and unmet needs.

Life's Sacred Seasons is a powerful spiritual and self-help guide that explores how to embrace each stage of life with wisdom, grace, and intention.

Ladies...If You Want A Man Than Read This!

This isn't another sugar-coated, "just be patient" dating book. In Ladies...If You Want A Man Then Read This!, Alice Truman serves up straight-up advice, laugh-out-loud truths, and eye-opening stories that will help you stop wasting time on the wrong ones - and finally attract the right one.

In **What Does Love Have To Do With The Money?**

relationship and self-help author Alice Truman breaks the silence on one of the toughest topics couples face: money and marriage. With honesty and practical guidance, she shows how couples can stop letting money divide them and start using it to build a stronger partnership.

When a Loved One Dies

This book gives you the clear, step-by-step answers you need. Written with both practicality and compassion, When a Loved One Dies is your essential guide for the critical hours, days, and weeks after loss.

Made in United States
Troutdale, OR
11/03/2026

56845406R00146